WITHDRAWN
UTSA LIBRARIES

The Pragmatic Mind

New Americanists   A Series Edited by Donald E. Pease

The

Pragmatic

Explorations in the Psychology of Belief

Mind

Mark Bauerlein

Duke University Press   Durham and London   1997

This research was supported in part by the

University Research Committee of Emory University.

© 1997 Duke University Press

Chapter 2 is a revised version of an essay titled "Henry James,

William James, and the Metaphysics of American Thinking" that

first appeared in *America's Modernisms: Revaluing the Canon,* ed.

Kathryne V. Lindberg and Joseph G. Kronick (Baton Rouge:

Louisiana State University Press, 1996); reprinted by permission.

All rights reserved

Printed in the United States of America on acid-free paper ∞

Typeset in Bembo and Scala Sans by Keystone Typesetting, Inc.

Library of Congress Cataloging-in-Publication Data appear on the

last printed page of this book.

Library
University of Texas
at San Antonio

to Sophia St. Thomas Lyman

Contents

Preface: Pragmatism and Criticism

Why is pragmatism such a prominent topic in the humanities today? Pragmatism does not constitute a discrete method of literary scholarship or cultural criticism, and it has yielded no pattern of textual interpretation that might be recognizably "pragmatic." Yet, despite its ostensible indifference to the interpretation of art and culture, pragmatism does seem to have infiltrated American criticism. In the last fifteen years, a pragmatic vocabulary of *belief, practice, habit, consequences, contingency,* and *community* has cropped up in the writings of some of the discipline's leading figures: Stanley Fish, Harold Bloom, Barbara Herrnstein Smith, Walter Benn Michaels, Frank Lentricchia, Richard Poirier, Cornel West, and Giles Gunn, to name a few. And only six years after the publication of Richard Rorty's *Philosophy and the Mirror of Nature* appeared what many consider the sign of a methodology's sanctification: an anthology.[1] Since then, several books and articles have materialized with titles suggesting that pragmatism now occupies an official place in American criticism and intellectual history. As Rorty says, the word *pragmatism* "names the chief glory of our country's intellectual tradition,"[2] and it is only natural that pragmatism and cultural and literary studies should form a joint critical enterprise.

The question is, In what way does a philosophy whose basic principles address issues of truth, concepts, and scientific inquiry, not sociocultural constructs like literature, relate to criticism? What is it about pragmatism that has appealed to critics and scholars of the last decade?

To determine the connection between pragmatism and criticism, we must first note that *pragmatism* now refers to an intellectual formation quite different from that of traditional pragmatism. In a word, *pragmatism* today signifies the *new pragmatism,* an intellectual movement deriving from Rorty, not Peirce, James, or Dewey. The latter thinkers remain largely unexamined by neopragmatists. Although Rorty devotes brief portions of his books to Dewey, Michaels has a sharp essay on Peirce, Lentricchia and Gunn have one on James, and West has short chapters on all three in his genealogy,[3] the point of their readings lies not in a clarification of each thinker's terms and arguments but in a derivation of critical practice from those arguments. This shift from analysis to activation is in keeping with neopragmatist motives, for neopragmatists are intellectual activists, not commentators. They wish to set pragmatic principles to work, to test their utility and liberality. The new pragmatists leave the detailed explication of Peirce et al. to history of philosophy scholars and intellectual historians.

Indeed, many new pragmatists ignore that reconsideration of the "old" pragmatism because they find that process already completed by Rorty. For scholars attracted to pragmatism's core ideas but untrained in the logical methods that Peirce and Dewey developed and the psychophysiological processes that James assumed, Rorty offers a clear presentation of pragmatism's contemporary significance. His version of pragmatism simplifies a complex and at times technical set of texts and propositions into a workable springboard for criticism. In Rorty's characterization, Peirce is quickly dismissed as a vestigial Kantian still enamored of the hope that science will steadily converge on an extrahuman reality. James is distilled down to the precious insight that a correspondence theory of truth mistakes the purpose of human inquiry and hinders our liberating awareness of the constructedness of all things. Dewey is celebrated as the prophet of liberal social thought and reconstruction in philosophy. The intricacies of their respective philosophies are sacrificed to the expediency of making pragmatism *new*—and rightfully so, for Rorty's pragmatism is not a scholarly project but a programmatic directive. His essays mark "attempts to draw consequences from a pragmatist theory about truth,"[4] not to reexamine that theory and its premises.

Whether Rorty misrepresents "old" pragmatism or whether his pragmatism withstands logical analysis is of no concern here. Suffice it to say that, when Rorty condenses pragmatism into a few clear consequences, pragmatism assumes a new shape, one able to service the needs of critics. Still, however, it is unclear how to get from Rorty's form of pragmatism to the practice of criticism. If pragmatism has nothing specific to say about genre, popular culture, canon formation, Milton, visual media, and so on, how does it relate to critical inquiry? Fish and Knapp and Michaels concede that their arguments have no necessary effect on interpretation in practice.[5] So, again, what simplifications does Rorty work on pragmatism that prove congenial to literary and cultural studies?

Rorty's pragmatism offers critics two things: first, a resolution to debates over the place and purpose of critical theory; and, second, a justification for making criticism into an instrument for social reform. The first benefit places criticism on surer methodological ground and puts to rest a set of theoretical cruxes. The second gives to criticism a political identity and a reengagement with social and ethical issues from which theory and formalism had abstracted criticism.

First, the theoretical settlement. Neopragmatism expels questions of theory from criticism with a blank methodological pronouncement. Instead of trying to determine once and for all which theory of literature and culture corresponds most accurately with the reality of literature and culture, which theory best serves the training of students, which theory is the most philosophically sound, and so on, neopragmatism affirms an entirely new characterization of theory per se. Defining *theory* as the Platonic-Kantian search for a set of universal principles that may apply to any situation, Rorty says, "Such theories are attempts to ground some element of our practices on something external to these practices."[6] In Knapp and Michaels's refinement of Rorty's formulation, theory "is the name for all the ways people have tried to stand outside practice in order to govern practice from without."[7] Theory strives to occupy an extrapractical, uncontingent starting point, to find a transcendent position from which to speculate freely on particulars and prescribe rules of interpretation of them. It takes its direction from the "Platonic urge to escape from the finitude of one's time and place, the 'merely conventional' and contingent aspects of one's life."[8] Repressing its own origins, theory is a rarefied form of bad faith, a spurious attribution of one's partial inferences to some extrahuman ground, be it God, Nature, or Essence.

The theoretical project is bound to fail because, to put it bluntly, there is no escaping contingency. We cannot transcend our own time and place; we cannot speak any languages but our own. And, for new pragmatists, this is not so much an ontological principle as a methodological one. In actual practice, any theory we conceive will bear traces of the conditions of its conception, and these traces will be not accidental remnants but basic structures of the theoretical product. As Rorty affirms, "No description of how things are from a God's-eye point of view, no skyhook provided by some contemporary or yet-to-be-developed science, is going to free us from the contingency of having been acculturated as we were."[9] The historical, social, and institutional determinations that make up our ac-culturation are the bases from which theorists launch their contentions. Because, as Fish says, theory "cannot help but borrow its terms and its contents from that which it claims to transcend, the mutable world of practice, belief, assumptions, and so forth,"[10] theory's pretensions to neu-trality and universality collapse.

Under pragmatism's withering exposition, theory shrinks into trivia. The structuralist controversies and the poststructuralist competitions of earlier times appear to be the polemical jockeying of critics puffing them-selves up as philosophers. Having been shown to rest on a false abstraction of theory from practice, the interpretive *aporias* with which Paul de Man concludes his essays no longer seem tragic or even interesting.[11] What in the mid-1970s was hailed as a brilliant theoretical performance becomes by the mid-1980s a tedious rehearsal of clichés. Now, neopragmatism claims, criticism commands a different ethos: not theoretical sophistica-tion, or savvy handling of concepts, but an active and open awareness of what literary analysis can do, what difference it can make in our lives. Consider Bloom's claim for his own critical practice in *Agon* (1982) and how it differs from his outlook in earlier works: "What is a poem *for* anyway? is to me the central question, and by the question I mean prag-matically what *is* the use of poetry or the use of criticism?"[12] The insertion of the pronoun *I* implies that Bloom's answers lay no claim to theoretical status but instead relate poetry's use to provisional satisfactions. That is the neopragmatic attitude countering the theorist's phony universalism.

Critical theory has no answer to the new pragmatism's attack. Once one accepts the pragmatist's definition of theory, one has no way to refute the antitheory deductions that follow. To defend themselves against neopragmatism's characterization, theorists must either (1) argue that there is an extrapractical position from which theory can work, (2) rejoin that theory does not claim an extrapractical privilege for itself, or (3) protest that neopragmatism's representation of theory is a caricature. Option 1 is unavailable because theory itself renounces any interpretive act that claims to be guided by extrapractical, disinterested ideals. Critical theory asserts that such abstractions repress the fact that interpretation is always more or less implicated in the context of its occurrence. Option 2 is impractical because, if theory relinquishes its extrapractical position, it becomes just another practice, one not theoretically prior to any other. Finally, option 3 is not professionally feasible because many new pragmatists are already acknowledged as masters of critical theory. If such luminaries embrace a pragmatic attitude, then theorists must acknowledge the seriousness of pragmatism's challenge.

As we have seen, the new pragmatism's critique rests on a basic notion of the relation of theory to practice. This criticism is found made to order in Rorty's writings. However, neopragmatists can also find ample arguments against theory as extrapractice in the very intellectual tradition from which critical theory takes its concepts and that runs from Hegel to Foucault. Although it often phrases its lines of thought more in terms of antiempiricism or antipositivism than antitheory, this Continental tradition likewise rejects the kind of abstract transpractice into which neopragmatism skillfully pigeonholes theory. Gunn admits that pragmatism "would never have been capable of revival if it had not seemed to complement . . . rather than contest that body of critical and theoretical thought already transmitted from the Continent." And Rorty says, "Pragmatists and Derrideans are, indeed, natural allies."[13]

So, given pragmatism's perceived resemblance to Continental thought, why do neopragmatists turn to pragmatism as the exclusive antidote to "theory hope"? This question leads to the second advantage that pragmatism offers: a justification for criticism fulfilling a political purpose. While post-Hegelian philosophy and pragmatism share a disdain for the theoretical point of view as a positivist myth, neither Barthes nor Derrida nor de Man nor American literary theorists influenced by them try to extrapolate an explicit political praxis from their brand of interpretation. For the most part, poststructuralist criticism remains focused on the text. It offers readings of writings, not political agendas.

But in contrast to Continental dialectics, Rorty's pragmatism is a philosophy explicitly political, an outlook that begins with political questions and does not see them as posterior to the analysis itself. To Rorty, the meaning of a concept lies in its consequences.

What underwrites this focus on concrete effects is pragmatism's displacement of the correspondence theory of truth. Against the premise that a statement is true insofar as it accurately represents what it represents, pragmatism holds that truth is a property that we ascribe to all statements that work, that facilitate some desired end.

The neopragmatist rejects the correspondence supposition. New pragmatism sweeps aside the correspondence theory not by logically analyzing it or refuting its ontological commitments or denying the existence of the world itself. New pragmatism substitutes a concept's use value for its truth value by doing just that—making the substitution. The new pragmatist abandons the ambition of true representation, gives up on trying to match words to the way things are. Rather than trying to disprove the opposite of correspondence theory, the new pragmatist submits a different and more advantageous set of terms and descriptions than those correspondence uses. Indeed, the new pragmatist does not even bother to argue with the correspondence thinker over the relative merits of their rival views. Rorty: "My strategy will be to try to make the vocabulary in which these objections [to pragmatism] are made look bad, thereby changing the subject, rather than granting the objector his choice of weapons and terrain by meeting his criticisms head-on."[14]

New pragmatists do not argue and counterargue. They make correspondence language look bad and pragmatic language look good. Instead of playing the argumentative game, new pragmatists overcome inquirers pursuing foundations by making up new rules of inquiry, new protocols of discussion.

No longer worried about anchoring their discourse to an entity or principle beyond history and language, new pragmatists enjoy a freedom to think in ways that correspondence had foreclosed. This is not to say that new pragmatists believe that one can think or say anything—that would be to arrogate to minds the very uncontingency that pragmatism decried. However, thinkers can enjoy some portion of freedom in assuming that, with truth being constructed, not discovered, they may direct their conclusions toward this or that desirable practice, not back to some binding, extrapractical reality. Correspondence demands one result, the new pragmatism whatever result can pragmatically be sustained against other demands and possibilities. Rorty and his followers ask not which language is the most truthful (a single-answer question) but rather which language is the most beneficial, knowing that benefits change all the time.

Herein lies the appealing political impulse of the new pragmatism. Whereas Nietzsche, Foucault, de Man, and others adopt many of the same antirepresentational ideas but then follow with a nihilistic assertion of the loss of transcendence, new pragmatism interprets antirepresentationalism as the happy foreground of a reconstruction of culture and criticism. Derrida and de Man too often yield only "undecidables" and *aporias,* metaphysical dilemmas that cannot be solved in terms of the text being read. The new pragmatism appreciates the revealing of such problems, knowing that their repression will only resurface later on in the interpretation. But the new pragmatism attributes those problems to *those* terms, not to language or thought per se. The next step is not to reiterate the problem, but to change the terms.

This is why Rorty characterizes pragmatism as a game of redescription, a conversation in flux. One need only choose in which direction to move the conversation. The new pragmatists make that political decision according to the politics that best reflects a philosophy that affirms no metaphysical hierarchies, that eschews all foundations and fixed truths: liberal pluralism. Admitting a kind of progress that is not teleological, a form of improvement that is not headed for some single purpose, liberal pluralism accepts the plurality of descriptions, the principle that some descriptions are better than others here but not there, now but not later. Pragmatism is liberal pluralism's method of inquiry. Since all metaphysical grounds are unavailable, the purpose of pragmatic redescription is, not to get closer to Truth, but to revise our vocabularies and reform our institutions along more liberal, less repressive lines, to put "cultural criticism and political engagement in the service of an Emersonian culture of creative democracy."[15] The only constraint on inquiry and expression in this "just and free society" envisioned by the new pragmatism is "letting its citizens be as privatistic, 'irrationalist,' and aestheticist as they please so long as they do it on their own time—causing no harm to others and using no resources needed by those less advantaged."[16]

The new pragmatism supplies the philosophical arguments needed to sanction pluralist attitudes and convert criticism into a liberal agenda. The new pragmatism's insistence on practice reengages literature and criticism with history and society, rendering the theorist's disinterested posture a fraudulent denial of political investments. It encourages criticism to become "the production of knowledge to the ends of power and, maybe, of social change."[17] The antitheoretical work is done. Criticism now has a new practice: redescription for the purpose of social amelioration. In eradicating correspondence habits, the new pragmatism instills criticism with a political mission and gives it a social import.

Indeed, in some political versions of pragmatism, Rorty himself comes under fire for conserving elements of bourgeois individualism that pragmatism should overcome. Lentricchia, West, and Gunn each accuse Rorty of a lingering humanism. Lentricchia thinks that Rorty's emphasis on edification of selves makes reform too much of a private matter and hinders the broad social change he envisions. West charges Rorty with "refusing to push his own project toward cultural and political critiques of the civilization he cherishes," with "circumscrib[ing] his ethnocentric posthumanism within a practical arena of bourgeois humanism." "Rorty's neopragmatism," West continues, "only kicks the philosophic props from under liberal bourgeois capitalist societies; it requires no change in our cultural and political practices." And Gunn says that Rorty's program is salutary but that "Rorty wants to keep these alterations within well-defined cultural and linguistic borders," the most strict border being Rorty's axiom that selves cannot "stand beyond language."[18]

In other words, Rorty maintains a notion of selfhood that does not abide by the revisions he counsels. In denying essences and provisionalizing all truths, these political pragmatists argue, Rorty rightfully should quit all subjective foundations. The self is an identity that must give way to pragmatic redescription. If not, then pragmatic political critique will be stultified by identity politics.[19] Only if flux, pluralism, and provisionality accompany conceptions of epistemological entities, be they private selves

or interpretive communities, will pragmatism evolve into its proper political form, namely, "genealogical accounts deployed as moral and political
weapons in social and ideological contestations with those who rule and
dominate the lives of most of us."[20]

However, these extensions of Rorty's antitheory, pluralistic ideas to the
sociopolitical sphere raise another question. In its effort to escape epistemological problems about self and mind and become an activist intellectual program, has neopragmatism actually purified itself of those problems? Rorty says that "the new pragmatism differs from the old in just two
respects. . . . The first is that we new pragmatists talk about language
instead of experience or mind or consciousness as the old pragmatists
did."[21] But, in truth, have the new pragmatists removed mind-oriented
concerns and statements from their arguments? One might consider this
question a political or historical one, but here I would ask it in the new
pragmatism's own terms. The new pragmatism wishes to reform critical
practice. But, if one of pragmatism's basic principles is that practice and
belief go hand in hand and that belief is a mental habit, a tendency to
interpret in a certain way, then, to change our practices, we must address
the mental habits and tendencies that go along with the old practices.
Connecting concepts and beliefs to practice and consequences does not
eradicate the former or cast them as mere theoretical figments. Every
concept has a practical meaning, and every practice has a conceptual counterpart. To say that every belief marks a tendency to act in a certain way is
to say that every habitual action marks a tendency to believe in a certain
way. (This does not imply one relation between this action and that concept, only that there is always *some* relation, some belief-practice connection.) So, if we wish to loosen our inquiries from the constraints of Truth,
then we must identify and discard the Truth beliefs that yielded the Truth
practices. To break the theoretical habit, we must dismantle the theoretical
mind-set. To espouse a shift in interpretive practices without broaching
the mental habits allied to the former will effect only a partial revision. To
promote pragmatic method without developing a pragmatic thinking is
inadequate.

Perhaps Rorty and others would regard the focus on beliefs as mental
habits to be a return to the old theory of knowledge epistemology that
pragmatism has left behind.[22] But, although Rorty correctly says that
pragmatism spurns the theory search, that does not mean that pragmatism

abandons all questions about mind. For example, West places his "emphasis on the political and moral side of pragmatism" and says that pragmatism "shuns any linguistic, dialogical, communicative, or conversational models and replaces them with a focus on the multileveled operations of power." But West also says that pragmatism's "common denominator consists of a future-oriented instrumentalism that tries to deploy thought as a weapon to enable more effective action."[23] How thought might work as a "weapon" is in part a question of cognition, one that a discussion of the morals and politics of pragmatism does not fully answer. To take another example, Posnock highlights pragmatism's call for "reconstructing liberalism's ideology of self as 'ready-made,' fixed in opposition to a monolithic abstraction called society."[24] But a change in the ideology of self does not mean that the self has changed and that cognitive questions have gone away. If pragmatism means a change in practice, which is to say a change in belief, which is to say a change in thinking, then we need more than an ideological substitution. As a final example, Gunn seems to recognize this need in the placement of *intellect* in his title and in his criticism of Rorty's linguistic boundaries of selfhood. But Gunn weakly phrases his argument in ethical and aesthetic terms, asserting above all "the heuristic value of art," its capacity to "lift us out of ourselves, or compel us into a new relation to ourselves."[25] How that transcendence and new knowledge might work is, again, a cognitive question that ethical and aesthetic analyses skirt. In sum, Rorty and his new pragmatist followers and critics wish to break free of epistemology, but their language still bears important vestiges of cognitive themes that remain unresolved.

This is not to say that the new pragmatists are wrong or wrongheaded, only that some epistemic issues are still unsettled in their work. I think that many of those concerns can be addressed by returning to the "old" pragmatists and their substantial writings on mind. The following chapters broach this cognitive side of pragmatism and lay out some concepts of pragmatic mind as found in Emerson, James, and Peirce. (I leave Dewey out only because his early writings on cognition largely presuppose a pragmatic consciousness as developed by James and because his extension of that pragmatic consciousness to other fields requires a book in itself.) They propose, not to refute the new pragmatism, but to supplement it, to extrapolate from Emerson, James, and Peirce an intellectual dimension that is, I think, necessary to the broad social and academic reforms that the new pragmatists hail. It is necessary, but it is overlooked. Even though early pragmatists talked of mind, cognition, thinking, inference, and perception all the time, rarely in new pragmatic writings does one find more than a casual reference to them. Nevertheless, in its initial development, pragmatism did propose concepts of mind that, I contend, were crucial to the old pragmatism's success as a coherent philosophy. Also, because many of the terms of new pragmatic discourse—*identity politics, humanism, intellect, interpretive communities*—imply cognitive notions, a concept of mind may in fact be crucial to the viability of new pragmatic reform. In that case, the new pragmatism may find in the old pragmatism concepts of mind that might strengthen its polemic, clarify its arguments over identity and politics, sharpen its positioning of individuals in social structures, and make it a more coherent and pragmatic way of thinking about things.

The Pragmatic Mind

Introduction

To many philosophers, one of the things that distinguishes pragmatism is that it makes traditional philosophical questions about being and knowledge depend on the philosopher's choice of language. In its critical role, pragmatism turns philosophical analysis away from assertions about the accuracy of notions of being and knowledge and toward an exegesis of the meaning of those notions within a given "language game," "linguistic framework," or "conversation." As to what *meaning* means, pragmatism's definition of it as whatever consequences or behaviors follow from believing in this or that idea is what differentiates pragmatism from other linguistic turns. In its therapeutic role, having extricated philosophical study from the pursuit of extralinguistic truth, pragmatism encourages inquirers to develop new ways of describing the world and its inhabitants. It affirms that, since description is not only a representation but also a construction, not only a picture but also a proposal, a better description will yield a better world and a better way of dealing with it. Although he does not use the term, Carnap adopts a pragmatic standpoint when he says, first, "The introduction of new ways of speaking does not need any theoretical justification because it does not imply any assertion of reality"; and, second, "The acceptance [of new linguistic forms] cannot be judged as being either true or false because it is not an assertion. It can only be judged as being more or less expedient, fruitful, conducive to the aim for which the language is intended."[1]

Carnap's emphasis on the acceptance of linguistic frameworks marks a distinction crucial to the pragmatic outlook. Pragmatism highlights the choice of language, the decision to accept one linguistic framework or another and to do so because it is conducive to specific, local aims. Pragmatism does not make language itself into a master entity, one that might serve as the ground of being, consciousness, or value. Pragmatism focuses on the particular language that notions of reality, truth, and meaning belong to, but not in order to constitute the linguistic form itself into the foundation of those notions. Rather, it takes language as the most opportune site of philosophical attention, the best place to judge the significance of an idea.

Now, in claiming to clarify and contextualize ideas, pragmatism does not automatically answer any questions. It merely shifts the focus of analysis away from a concept's relation to a preconceptual reality and toward the way it works in a methodological framework, specifically, toward how it functions in organized situations. In giving priority to pragmatics over reference, pragmatists explicate the linguistic framework, not to test accuracy but to clarify its implications, to sharpen its intension, to mark its limits. As Quine puts it, pragmatic analysis has "the task of making explicit what had been tacit, and precise what had been vague; of exposing and resolving paradoxes, smoothing kinks, lopping off vestigial growths, clearing ontological slums."[2] Pragmatists draw out all the implicit relations, all the unremarked assumptions and latent concepts haunting every statement and sometimes proving destructive to the aim at hand. They examine a representation's formal clarity and pragmatic utility, not its adherence to the structure of nature. The latter is the scientist's job (which the pragmatist would like to complement). While the empirical scientist observes and calculates the object in order to correct his description of it, the pragmatist analyzes the description itself in an effort to improve it, to give it greater simplicity and effectiveness.

That way, pragmatism purges language of useless verbiage and contradictory meanings and yields a better way of handling the world. What *better* signifies remains a matter of debate. Indeed, in every issue that arises, that is the pragmatic question, and, although the answer to it will have remedial effects, it must be different each time since each situation entails different aims and constraints. To ask and answer a question pragmatically, then, the questioner must revise his or her definitions and conceptions. An inquirer must hold off from elevating the things signified by the new description into *the* guide to description. Various new experiences may compel redescription, but pragmatists make those adjustments in how to conceive and investigate them without believing in them unconditionally. In thinking and acting pragmatically, inquirers approach problem solving in local terms, as the fulfillment of specific aims. A reality is established, but the reality on which one settles remains specific to the needs of the inquiry that assumed or produced it.

Why is this so? Why is it that, as Moore, Russell, Bergson, and other early commentators on pragmatism quickly noted, the success of pragmatism rests on the displacement of correspondence as a guiding philosophical motive? Because correspondence thinking presupposes a correspondent, a reality to which words should adhere. It destines inquiry to one result that is true and considers anything like pragmatic judgment to rest shakily on an unsustainable relativism. So, to feel justified in adjusting the terms and methods of analysis and description, to treat the pragmatic selection of one language over another not as a violation of the way things really are, one must subordinate language's objective reference to its practical or conceptual usefulness, its capacity to yield good results or to make our ideas clear. Inquirers must break the habit of committing themselves ontologically to their conclusions and develop a disposition that entails only methodological commitments. Inquirers must learn to say, not "This is true," but "This works." To make that translation abiding, to keep truth (as correspondence) from sliding back into the research project, pragmatists must embrace a frame of mind that incorporates choice into its very makeup, that directs attention, not toward objects waiting to be recorded accurately as knowledge, but toward the variety of available starting points for conceiving objectivity in the first place.

However, to speak of pragmatism in this way is to employ a language positing something else besides a methodological axiom of choice. That language suggests that withholding ontological commitments requires more than a mere procedural decision. The terms I have used—*frame of mind, thinking, inclination, disposition*—imply that curtailing the desire to say that our terms invariably denote unconceptualized objective entities involves a basic change in mental outlook. The call to break the correspondence habit—*habit* here signifying a cognitive pattern—presupposes that there is a pragmatic mentality distinct from a correspondence mentality, a pragmatic ego or intelligence that underlies pragmatic study. This is to say, not that pragmatic mentality is radically different from correspondence mentality, but only that the two operate through some contrasting cognitive habits. In this case, given the postulate that every practice has its cognitive side, then pragmatism's principles of expedience, fruitfulness, and satisfaction must apply both to a method of analysis and to a manner of cognition of the things analyzed. If, as pragmatism stipulates, the meaning of an idea lies in whatever practical consequences follow from believing in it, then there must be some direct connection between belief and consequences, idea and act, conception and method.

Here is the point of this study: to clarify that relation of method and mind. The argument is motivated by the questions, Does pragmatism affirm any cognitive habits as necessary to the pragmatic method? Does pragmatism imply a distinctive attitude of mind?

The book answers these questions not through a conceptual analysis of mind or a determination of the relation between cognition and inquiry. It offers a scholarly discussion of the term *pragmatic mind* and does so by extrapolating a notion of pragmatic mind from selected arguments and assertions made by America's early pragmatists: Ralph Waldo Emerson, William James, and Charles Sanders Peirce. The arguments analyze pragmatic mind and try to deduce the conceptual background of the term, strictly within the context of those thinkers' work. More specifically, this book serves as a commentary on those texts—mainly, Emerson's *Nature,* "The Method of Nature," and "Plato; or, The Philosopher"; James's "The Sentiment of Rationality" and *Principles of Psychology;* and Peirce's so-called cognition papers and "How to Make Our Ideas Clear"—that present and/or explicate a method of thinking that complements a pragmatic method of inquiry.

Of course, deriving a notion of pragmatic cognition, reasoning, judgment, and so on from these nineteenth-century American essays and treatises does not settle whether the concept is meaningful, useful, and free of psychologistic or mentalistic fallacies. Nor does a scholarly commentary on these early pragmatists' concept of mind argue for a necessary connection between a certain form of cognition and pragmatic inquiry. Nor does it determine whether epistemological concepts are necessary to any characterization of pragmatic inquiry. What it does do is demonstrate the role that a conception of mind plays in the conceptual field out of which pragmatism evolves. It uncovers in the writings of Emerson, James, and Peirce a close relation between method and mind and finds a notion of pragmatic cognition at the root of the famed pragmatic method. In their philosophical canons, before expounding their pragmatic maxims, James and Peirce both attempt lengthy descriptions of how mind works. Before outlining pragmatic theories of truth and methods of inquiry, each philosopher develops a sophisticated model of cognition, James preferring to do so by experimental observation, Peirce by logical inference. Likewise, although he counts as a pragmatist only insofar he anticipates many later pragmatic formulations, Emerson consistently initiates his essays with the proposition that a reform of mind's "angle of vision," of its transcendental activity, is the prerequisite for any practical reform. Indeed, in renouncing the wholesale division of intellect and action, in defining thought as intellectual action, Emerson asserts that every cognitive alteration that mind makes instantaneously brings about a change in the world that mind inhabits.

This book attempts to develop these and other conceptual connections between pragmatic method and pragmatic mind—again, exclusively within the context of Emerson's, James's, and Peirce's works. That is the total framework under scrutiny here.

Investigating the genesis of pragmatism suggests a historical inquiry, but the kind of genesis I am thinking of here has to do with a structure of ideas, not a structure of events. Specifically, this book traces the evolution of pragmatic method out of numerous assumptions, definitions, and inferences involving a notion of pragmatic mind. It strives to compensate for the narrowness of its concerns with a more detailed exploration of pragmatism's initial conceptual field than broad chronicles of American thought make room for. While comprehensive studies of nineteenth-century American philosophy and intellectual history (such as those by Herbert W. Schneider, Bruce Kuklick, Elizabeth Flower and Murray Murphey, and H. S. Thayer) provide fuller representations of the socio-historical background and cultural climate of pragmatism, this book sets out to reconstruct in more conceptual detail the relation of mind to method and show how it partakes in the advent of pragmatism.[3]

Chapter One

Thinking in the Emersonian Way

The opening paragraph of Emerson's *Nature* has often been taken as a definitive description of the American thinker's situation. Its diagnostic pronouncements of "retrospection," "original relation," "insight," "tradition," "nature," and so on have induced literary scholars to tease out of American Renaissance writings a uniquely American sociohistorical aesthetic, a "literary democracy" that asks American writers to assume a certain posture toward the past, present, and future.[1] Emerson's epigrams articulate a historical and political directive, requiring that Americans adopt an oppositional relation to any ossified social structure—be it Europe, Christianity, America's colonial past, or the Harvard curriculum—and proceed to "demand [their] own works and laws and worship" (*CW*, 1:7).[2] Because "there are new lands, new men, new thoughts" awaiting a new expression (not just an expression of their newness), American artists are faced with accomplishing a double originality, which is to say, with maintaining a double antagonism. On the one hand, they must counteract those creeping social institutions and personal habits that both delimit the field of expression and domesticate any revelation into conventional social practices. On the other, they must resist any backward-looking attitude that absorbs all face to face beholdings of God and nature into customary genres and obscures the radical content of that "insight" in discussions of taste, rules, and ornament.

This New World mandate requires that self-reliant citizens implant themselves at an inaugural metaphysical threshold: when the natural present gets translated into a social past. Because the latter tends to displace the former or to represent the former only in institutionalized repetitions, individuals must hearken again and again to nature—not, however, to *be* natural, to live a nonsocial, nonhistorical existence (Emerson disdains such naïvetés), but to maintain an "original *relation* to the universe," a fruitful interplay of spirit and nature, of humanized forms and native forces. American "representative men" must inhabit a precarious nature-culture transition, an ideal first historical moment that initiates the memorializing tendency yet clings to the natural "floods of life stream[ing] around and through us."[3] Americans produce "action proportioned to nature," drawing primal power into a human world, an age, but abandoning that social formation the instant it forsakes its original relation and becomes (in the hands of "conformists") related only to its application to various social events. Daily answering nature's restless invitation, whose "every hour and change corresponds to and authorizes a different state of mind" (*CW,* 1:9), Americans should dwell at the site of the "new." And living in perpetual renewal is not just a matter of attaining a unique experience, of undergoing elemental, unmediated apprehensions of nature. The idea of mediation as an inescapable human condition occurs too frequently in Emerson for us to identify originality with immediacy. Instead, the new happens when we discover different and better relations with nature, when we transform these currently foreign relations into "an occult relation" that gives "greatest delight" (p. 10).

For this reason, to characterize Emerson's imperative as a blank anti-historicism is to interpret his project somewhat one-sidedly as a politics of individualism.[4] If this Emersonian attitude were simply a matter of opposition, of an individual American mind rejecting a tradition or institution, then American innovation would amount to a mere substitution of beliefs—democracy for aristocracy, nature for convention, "revelation" for "history." American revisionary action would involve a revaluing of individual experience over traditionalized experience in the name of an ethical principle: the inalienable right to originality. But antihistoricism, individ-ualism, and nativism merely abolish that which tradition, retrospection, and history preserve. Antihistoricism therefore imports simply an inver-sion of already established values, not a genuine interrogation of the mean-ing and genesis of those values. The conception of tradition and individu-ality, the thinking of their relation to self, society, and nature, remains the same in either case.

Although these are fairly commonplace political observations, it is im-portant to appreciate the cognitive dimension of Emerson's proposal. His promptings call for a transvaluation *and* a new cognition of the things valued: not only a new object of experience but a new *mode* of experience, a "new thought." Retrospection is a guiding mental habit, a cognitive attitude determining one's relation to the past and present universes. Therefore, escaping the historical passivity that retrospection imposes on us rests on the possibility of realizing a different cognitive attitude. Emer-son solicits a method of mind in harmony with nature's temporality, not history's chronology. If prospection is to rescue the living generation from routine imitations of the past, it must perform something other than the flip side of retrospection, other than an opposite looking. Here is Emer-son's insight: respect for original relation. Mind should heed the volatility of tradition-insight, history-revelation oppositions and treat the choice of one term over the other as an impoverishment of experience. An either/ or choice narrows experience too much, commits mind to a single course of thinking, a traditional one or a revelatory one. Shunning that foolish consistency, an Emersonian mind cultivates a buoyant mental posture, regards its successive cognitions not as confirmations of a prior choice, but as experiments in living.

In the words of *Nature*'s second paragraph, Emersonian thinking lives in "curiosity," an "apprehension" that poses "questions" and makes "in-quiries" (*CW,* 1:7) but eschews the quick conclusion, the easy answer (which is what tradition supplies). Indeed, it is the inquiries, not the answers, that reveal "man's condition."[5] For a question is not a sign of ignorance or uncertainty. Though it wants an answer, a question also predetermines the shape of the answer and this implicit conditioning no answer can exceed (only another question can do that). The question is a "solution in hieroglyphic." That "we have no questions to ask which are unanswerable" (p. 7) implies that every inquiry already determines the form of its resolution—that is, distinguishes what counts as relevant, what gets recognized as related.[6] An empirical answer indicates an empirical question, an empiricist's thinking. A particular curiosity is always answered through a particular angle of vision. So, to get to the bottom of human curiosity, to answer the riddle of the Sphinx, we need more than just an answer. Rather, we require an exploration of that which awakens curiosity in the first place, namely, nature—"Let us interrogate the great apparition. . . . Let us inquire, to what end is nature?"

Why nature and not God, man and woman, knowledge, society? First, because nature seems to be the raw material out of which individuals build their own worlds. Second, because nature functions to strip thinking of all "mean egotism," to render all "names," "acquaintances," "streets and villages" "foreign and accidental," "a trifle and a disturbance" (*CW,* 1:10). While the other terms mentioned above fall too easily into institutional forms (God as the church, man and woman as marriage, knowledge as the academy, society as the gentleman's club, the charitable organization, or the political party), nature by definition remains opposed to all institutions. Keeping nature in mind, individuals prevent themselves from being exhausted by social and political engagements. Inquiring into nature is how individual thinkers mark the limits of human being. Purifying personalities, politicians, servants, and slaves into "transparent eye-balls," "the woods" breaks down that benign passivity that institutions instill in their members and prepares American minds for a redemptive receptivity to new thoughts and new experiences. Although such moments may not happen often, when they do, nature inspires a reverent curiosity about being, the most congenial epistemic stance for knowing ourselves and our meanings.

Taking its direction from nature and applying its thinking to its own activity, this thoughtful interrogation surpasses an epistemological framework whereby knowledge gets categorized into ways of knowing, a category not entirely new. That approach defines experience as a one-way movement from either nature to mind or vice versa. If an inquiry takes nature as simply a material object with which mind works, it neglects an essential constituent of the original relation out of which human being emerges, mistaking mind for an in itself, a self-originating substance projecting its ways of knowing in versions of art and science. On the other hand, if an inquiry takes nature as a dynamic participant in experience but does not query the angle of the inquiry's own curious vision, it fails to recollect mind's initial objectification of nature, the limitation of nature to suit the question. That forgetfulness yields a narrow-minded positivism, "an addition or subtraction or other comparison of known quantities" (*CW,* 1:39). Also, taking the objectification of nature for granted takes the subjectification of thinking for granted—a weak relaxation of curiosity, for objectification and subjectification mark a simultaneous constitution of the one and the other, this constitution being the operation each one-sided inquiry ignores. Of course, with a static subject-object distinction established, such partial epistemologies do have benefits. They quicken the progress of scientific knowledge, bring the knower and the known to-gether in a growing storage of facts. But they also have drawbacks: no longer "an awaken[ed] . . . mind," the knower proceeds confidently in a familiar objective terrain, middlingly edified by the experiment. And, no longer "nature . . . describing its own designs," the known becomes an object of observation, distanced from "the colors of the spirit" (p. 10).

It is precisely these substantiations before which Emersonian thinking hesitates. It asks if there is a thinking before subjectivity, a nature before objectivity, if there is some relation more original than that of subject-object. And, knowing that all worldly relations are largely mapped out in the asking, that an empirical discovery unveils not a new relation but only a related empirical term, Emersonian thinking prefers not to end its inquiry, pauses before each tantalizing answer. When it does move forward, when it apprehends a "new thought," envisions a "new land," or recognizes "new men," Emersonian inquiry works by posing the question "to what end is nature?" and announcing what the answer might look like. So, while the second paragraph ends with the nature question, the third paragraph proceeds to state how one way of thinking—"science"—would go about answering it:

> All science has one aim, namely, to find a theory of nature. We have theories of races and of functions, but scarcely yet a remote approxima-tion to an idea of creation. We are now so far from the road to truth, that religious teachers dispute and hate each other, and speculative men are esteemed unsound and frivolous. But to a sound judgment, the most abstract truth is the most practical. Whenever a true theory appears, it will be its own evidence. Its test is, that it will explain all phenomena.

Now many are thought not only unexplained but inexplicable; as language, sleep, dreams, beasts, sex. (*CW,* 1:8)[7]

Beginning by positing a "theory of nature" as a result, this solicitous paragraph seems to espouse "theory" as the pathway to "truth," the corrective instrument that would bring thought and opinion back from the "unsound and frivolous." With a sound "idea of creation" in hand, "dispute and hate" would dissolve into concordance and love, and "religious teachers" would properly act as prophets, not polemicists. Instead of leading speculation into fruitless, sterile abstraction and away from "Commodity," "Beauty," "Language," and "Spirit," a "true theory" would be a "Discipline," would generate action, reform, "worship," and other "Prospects." While various superficial "theories of races and of functions" effect only a factitious relation (because, one might assume, they are bound to the finite "understanding"), this "true theory" would unriddle the human "hieroglyphic" and, paradoxically, propel American thinkers forward into new possibilities of thought and backward to every thought's vital beginnings.

Given these beneficent results, the question then becomes not one of theory per se, but one of truth: How is one to know which theory is true, is fact? What can be the basis of discrimination? Fully aware that his criterion must be extra- or pretheoretical, Emerson's "science" contends that what confirm this theory as true are both its self-evidence and its explanatory capacity. Its authority rests in its intuitive appeal (whereby its truth strikes the soul) and its empirical facility (its universal applicability). It simultaneously meets the contrary demands of the idealist's reflection and the naturalist's experimentation. Being "its own evidence," a "true theory" transcends debate, argument, verification. It makes "the most abstract truth" into "the most practical" activity. Converting frivolous speculation into community action, bridging that problematic epistemological gap between word and thing, sign and meaning, theory and practice, and rationalizing those metaphysical differences (over questions of freedom, faith, death) that instigate controversy and confusion, "true theory" is self-legitimizing. If it were not, if it required proof or illustration for legitimacy, then it would rely on the relations (of correspondence, of abstract-concrete, of rule-example) that it purports to explain. Hence, by definition, "true theory" requires no references: as it is conceived, it happens; as it is realized, it works.

But to say that true theory has an immediate, universal effect, that it lays bare reality and mind, is, strictly speaking, to say that it has no application, that it is its own practice, its own meaning. It dispenses with any follow-up procedures. Again, if it did not, then that procedure itself would have to be accounted for, would have to be corroborated by another theory, a theory of the true theory. This is why true theory produces a total and terminal event. Explaining everything equally everywhere, it compels a constant invocation, in so doing annihilating the structure of invocation. It is not brought to bear on persons, things, or nature, for persons and things and nature are the outcome of "true theory's" simplifying action. "True theory" discharges the possibility of human projection, explanation, interpretation. There is no pretheory world on which to be projected, for the projection is the world, and every world encountered as not your projection is someone else's projection (reified into "tradition," the fathers' "sepulchres").[8]

So the whole notion of legitimacy or confirmation, of a secondary testing, is irrelevant to it—it simply is true. "True theory" justifies—it needs no justification. Peremptorily setting all other theories to rest, it commands immediate assent. It "explain[s] all phenomena," thus restoring to the world its candor and lucidity. A true theory does not curtail mind's inquiries into nature, but rather opens nature to mind's curiosity, makes nature into a limpid window to Spirit, a resplendent viewpoint congenial to the visionary's vision. At this point, nature is not composed of phenomena—it is immanence. Henceforth, mind does not interpret: it sees.

What the Emersonian scientist hopes to find in his search for total explanation and "simplicity and truth" (*CW*, 1:30) is a theory to end theorizing—a theory that would bring us face to face with nature and transform each individual into a representative visionary. While some inquirers would covet that theory as an ultimate solution, an end to speculation and vision, the Emersonian scientist implements that theory to put skepticism and alienation to rest and free mind for new cognitions of the universe. Object-oriented science wants a theory that will reduce human thinking to routine attachments to demystified objects (which are, in Emerson's thinking, despiritualized objects). Emersonian science wants a theory that will reveal the demystification of nature as but one possible direction of experience. It seeks a theory in whose context demystification will mark but one relation that mind has to the universe.

Emerson wishes to avoid a science that allows for only one experiential attitude—"objectivity"—an attitude that develops at the expense of spirit. Or, if it acknowledges spirit, objectivity reduces spirit to mere immaterial substance. It limits experience to a single relation, one original perhaps in Newton's time but restrictive in our age. To correct that impoverishment, Emersonian thinking tries to posit another relation, a new set of experiential terms and distinctions. It yields original and better relations, and it also remains attentive to the relation-making process, the latter being the proper haunt of spirit. An Emersonian theory of nature not only proposes "theories of races and of functions," models of human beings and their tools. It also strives toward "an idea of creation," a concept of conception adequate to spirit's capacity to evolve. This is why there is no one true theory. Spirit is creation, not created. Any particular relation that claims to exhaust spirit's potential makes the perverse claim of comprehending that which gives rise to it in the first place. A "true theory" and its idea of creation underscores the partiality of any created relation—not in order to condemn relatedness per se, but in order to explode any single relation's claim to privilege and to allow spirit a freer exercise in the world.

That is Emerson's desire, to theorize mind into a flexible, spiritual self-reliant activity that forges ahead with its "original relation"—construction business. Theory must remain an initiating idea of creation and not become one created idea among many others, or else it will confine spirit to one theoretical product. If it is to inspire thinking, an idea of creation must differ from normal ideas, precisely in that it must constitute not a content but a mental disposition, an approach to the world. As a stabilizing preparation, a nascent arrangement of motives, ideas, and interests into one solid ground (among many possible others), "true theory" is an enabling but transitional moment, a provisional concession to abstract thinking that translates quickly into positive action.

This remedial but forward-looking strategy implements theory to suspend that which enables theory to transpire: "secondary relations," opacity, the non-"coincident" status of "the axis of vision" and "the axis of things." Theory repairs the curious and lamentable dislocation of "Me" from "Not Me," the mental disjunction that converts vision into perception, belief into interpretation. It obviates the moment of skepticism, doubt, recalcitrance, when, pausing on "the discovery we have made that we exist" (*CW*, 3:43), mind succumbs to one of its most subversive, self-defeating activities—introversion. Introversion halts the course of action with its own debilitating reaction, distorts the force of genius into a specular navel gazing. An introverted mind thinks that it relates only to itself—it fetishizes its experiences with nature into subjective variations of impression, mood, memory. It is true that in "The American Scholar," after stating, "Our age is bewailed as the age of Introversion," Emerson asks, "Must that needs be evil?" (*CW*, 1:66) and goes on to suggest that introversion proves a worthy alternative to conformity. But that means that introversion is just a reaction to socialization, not a creative gesture in itself.

This explains why, when outside a degraded social context, introversion marks a crippled mind. Hence, "We have invincible repugnance to introversion," Emerson writes in *Natural History of Intellect* (which explores the fall into self-consciousness through several pages), for "the natural direction of the intellectual powers is from within outward," and "a study in the opposite direction had a damaging effect on the mind." An "inward analysis" (*W*, 12:13–14) constitutes mind as a self-contained object, a thing to scrutinize in isolation, its isolation only aggravated by intellect's narcissistic gaze. Poring over an already objectified mind, introspection fails to understand its own activity, for the essential originality of introversion lies, not in the results of its inward observations, but in the constitution of mind as an object to observe. But, then, the latter enabling act is precisely what introversion forgets, and this forgetfulness of its most creative moment is introversion's pitfall. Looking at mind as object, indeed, as an object dislocated from natural objects, introversion casts mind and nature as face to face (or back to back) in an original *dis*relation. Apart from overlooking the fact that disrelation still falls in the category of relation, introversion errs in treating mind as a subjective object opposing objective objects, whereas it rightfully should regard subjective objectivity as but one of mind's possible manifestations. But, then, that is precisely what introversion cannot do.

This suppression has "damaging effects." Threatening to enervate Power and Instinct, to turn Intellect into a channel of abuse and impotence, "This slight discontinuity which perception effects between the mind and the object paralyzes the will" (*W*, 12:44). "Introversion" broods on the relation, connection, or, rather, disconnection of subject and object and thereby degenerates into a metaphysics of self-involvement, a hallucinatory practice whereby a subject becomes an object to itself. That is, interested more in rumination than action, forgetting that "metaphysics is dangerous as a single pursuit" (p. 13), self-scrutiny originates only a self to scrutinize. As a "single" endeavor, the introverted intellect feeds on its own uncertainties, treats uncertainty itself as a thing to play with rather than as a "mental mood" to deliberate on and to surpass. Although Emerson, in his own description, "writes anecdotes of the intellect; a sort of Farmer's Almanac of mental moods," the intellect has a task to perform beyond its own perpetuation: "My metaphysics are to the end of use" (pp. 11, 13).

To make metaphysics useful, "Thought must take the stupendous step of passing into realization" (*W,* 12:43) and thereby become, not merely a thinking about, but a thinking put into effect.[9] "If the thought is not a lamp to the will, does not proceed to an act, the wise are imbecile" (p. 46), foolishly absorbed in a labyrinth of epistemological *aporias.* Emerson's theory bridges the interval of will and representation, the divisions of self-consciousness, and the vacillations of reflexivity—in a word, it eradicates the conditions of theoretical speculation. After true theory has adjusted mind to common sense and sound judgment, knowledge of an impractical, dualistic theoretical kind is unnecessary, even impertinent, especially considering nature's utter immanence: "The tree or the brook has no duplicity, no pretentiousness, no show" (p. 54). With true theory presiding over the universal simplicity of life as it is, everything is always already in its place, ready not only for scientific study and technological use, should they happen to be desired, but also for vision and worship. Whether this marks an original relation is an open question, but, in any case, the hazards of speculation have evolved into visionary certainty, self-absorption has become mental expansion.

Emersonian theory works only in order to efface itself. Once theory has performed its unifying function, it has obliterated its subject matter and discharged its raison d'être. The path has been cleared of all tired conventions, mind has been disabused of introversion, and Americans may now convert thinking into action. The necessity of interpretation has given way to a reign of wonder. The nature that once lay dormant beneath timeworn conceptions now appears as the authentic ground of a new history. Henceforth, American thinkers may brood intellectually on a panorama of new material and spiritual lands. They may act their thoughts as innovations, secure in the momentary rightness of their conceptions, untroubled by the old derivative dualisms and doubts.

This is why even true theory is merely provisional, an organization for action, not a judge of action. True theory exists only so long as false theory misguides humanity, only so long as the barren contraries truth and falsity displace the progressive contraries active and paralyzed, original and derivative. Falsely theorized minds persist in regarding nature as a foreign substance they must serve or suffer, a "phenomenon perfect" for another, not "for you" (*CE*, 1:44). So they cling to the prevailing, reiterated interpretation of things, the certified paradigm securing mind from the fear and trembling of making nature over in another image. Their aims turned inward by uncertainty, their force disabled by conformity, maladjusted minds fall prey to "Imbecility" and become "victims of gravity, custom, and fear," possessing "no habit of self-reliance or original action" (*W*, 6:54). True theory overrides mind's crippling self-mistrust, rids mind of that parasitic un-Montaigne-like skepticism generating retrospective anxieties, and fosters that anxious but healthy "interrogation of custom" that "is an inevitable stage in the growth of every superior mind" (*W*, 4:172).

However, true theory empowers mind not by reassuring mind of its truth, its correspondence with objects, but rather by awakening mind to its own powers and possibilities, its "divinity." Again, if true theory were to provide a knowledge, a principle, a truth rarefied into a set axiom, then true theory would amount only to an addition of content to mind's store of ideas. There would be no qualitative or formal difference between true and false, the predications right and wrong would still apply, and the twofold structure of verification (hypothesis-proof, theory-practice) would therefore remain in effect. Mind would remain cognitively unchanged, although it would achieve a substitution of correct knowledge for incorrect knowledge.

But, instead of resolving the enigma of nature with an answer, instead of satisfying mind's desire to know nature perfectly by offering up the perfect representation of things, "true theorizing" aspires to reorient the manner of mind's interrogation, to adjust the organizing structures and conditions of its knowledge. In the hands of an Emersonian thinker, true theory breaks down the popular mind-set, the regnant cognitive map, and thereby limits what is considered ordinary, immediate, unmistakable experience.

True theory critiques those preconceptions misleading mind into acquiescence, into being imposed on by its own unrecognized actions. It tries to
lift mind out of its present imposition, to reverse the decay of creative
intelligence into passive observation.

In a word, a misled mind, a consciousness unknowingly abiding by the
customary ways of seeing, accepts the givenness of sensation. The fallen
mind's eye is a mere receiver, not an artist. In that condition, Emerson says
in *Nature,* the inevitability and external priority of sensation pass unquestioned before "the unrenewed understanding['s] . . . instinctive belief in
the absolute existence of nature" (p. 30). Against that observational aver-
age, that herd perception, true theory proposes a general accounting of
immediacy, givenness, absolute reality, and any other extrahuman ground
of experience. It takes those givens as subtle but coercive institutions, static
tools of conformity portraying themselves as the natural attitude. That
base of perception may at one time have been a unique, original inspiration, but, through influence and repetition, through the dispersal of individual vision into collective will, perception decayed into a "despotism of
the senses" (p. 30). And then, knowing how the nonhuman always seems
to own a certain truth claim that the human never possesses, that despotic
attitude authorized itself (through its doctrinaires) by repressing its autho-
rization, by concealing any human decisions on which it rested. It denied
its own origination, withdrew itself from any visionary wellspring.

To loosen from the current vision of things its dogmatic, insistent title
to reality, to see the things themselves once again as vision, true theory
destroys the attitude of passivity, the Lockean paradigm of knowledge.[10] It
dismantles the supposedly inalterable progress from extension and motion
to the senses to the understanding by postulating other possibilities of
experience, by releasing thinking, believing, from the purview of the
empirical tradition. After true theory's redemptive adjustment, Emerson
writes in "Fate," an essay written several years after *Nature* but still pondering the same question of thought's relation to action, "Thought dissolves
the material universe by carrying the mind up into a sphere where all is
plastic" (*W,* 6:28). Nature's indurate character becomes a passing moment
in an ever-hardening and -softening "plasticity," in an extravagating history of "thought, of the spirit which composes and decomposes nature,"
which battles the "limitation" "we popularly call Fate" (pp. 22, 20). Or, in
more explicitly political terms, the "material universe" is ultimately re-

vealed to be a tool of coercion, one of the many "torrents of tendency" so subtly widespread that any questioning of it "looks so ridiculously inadequate that it amounts to little more than a criticism or protest made by a minority of one, under compulsion of millions" (p. 19).

Seeing that fatal hardening as a social domestication of vision, mind recovers its "stupendous antagonism" (*W,* 6:22).[11] Then knowledge is not so much a matter of Fate, of mind being directed toward a particular truth, as it is a conflict of Fate (the established truth) and Power (an incipient truth coming into form). Or, rather, knowledge is a trial of Powers, for what is Fate but some institution's solidified Power? And this contest of faculties is decided, not by truth, but by force. When two persons encounter one another, "There is a measuring of strength, very courteous but decisive, and an acquiescence thenceforward when these two meet. . . . The weaker party finds that none of his information or wit quite fits the occasion. . . . But if he knew all the facts in the encyclopedia, it would not help him; for this is an affair of presence of mind, of attitude, of aplomb" (p. 59).

This is not simply a statement of might makes right, of political tyranny obfuscating the truth into propaganda or recasting a political state of affairs as the natural course of things. That truth or state is already a function of Power, not some raw material that Power adapts to its designs. For, to Emerson, nothing exists without support. Nothing can come from nothing. "Presence of mind" implies that that support is right there to be seen and felt, that it "strengthens" by direct, explicit force, not by an appeal to abstract principles, which are simply "old" forces ossified into routine perceptions and "encyclopedic" facts. And what gives a particular vision of things authority is not only the personal strength of the visionary but also the personal strength that that vision evokes in others, their recognition of their own strength returning "with a certain alienated majesty" (*CW,* 2:27) in the representative woman's or man's utterance. Ideally, the measure of Power is inspiration, not how much that Power repeats itself through others, but how much that Power inspires others to surpass it. The most powerful Power applies itself to its own annihilation, cancels its dominion by breeding the Power that supersedes it: "We hear eagerly every thought and word from an intellectual man. But in his presence our own mind is roused to activity, and we forget very fast what he says, much more interested in the new play of our thought than in any thought of his" (*W,* 6:26).

So what mind desires is a "new play of our thought." Truth is an immobility, correspondence a treadmill. In "Experience," Emerson says only a lightsome elasticity of thinking can save minds from the "chain of physical necessity" and the imbecility of unconscious imitation, can abandon that leaden determinism and "live amid surfaces, [where] the true art of life is to skate well on them" (*CW,* 3:32, 35).[12] Later, in "Fate," we read that a representative man or woman proves that "every solid in the universe is ready to become fluid on the approach of the mind, and the power to flux it is the measure of the mind" (*W,* 6:43). He or she arrives to clear the ground, to "flux" a society's grooved impressions and open it to a new expression of Power.

But, as "Fate" would have it, every "fluidity" is destined for "solidity," for "the truth is in the air, and the most impressionable brain will announce it first, but all will announce it a few minutes later" (*W,* 6:43, 44). And, as soon as the "they" adopt it, as soon as the first announcement expands into law, into a repeatable, anonymous principle, the "truth" petrifies. This is the inevitable declension of vision: from original conception to habitual perception. First gratifyingly received as a colossal reshaping of an outworn world, on its common acceptance, vision passes into disposition, into a benign lethargy of works and days. What was understood as a new way of looking at things is now casually treated as the things themselves, as the given world divorced from any single perspective. At that point, as one avid reader of Emerson asserts, "*What is truth?*—Inertia; that hypothesis which gives rise to contentment; smallest expenditure of spiritual force, etc."[13] No matter how explanatory or curative that truth once was, no matter how much it may have reawakened the stupefied senses of the passive majority, once vision achieves a state of rest, it dissipates into observation: "The truest state of mind rested in becomes false" (*W,* 12:60).

In its properly active mode, mind is motion, or, rather, mind is a sequence of visionary flights and momentary arrests. Ever in transit, when mind hits on a satisfying explanation, a revivifying vision, it enjoys a merely provisional repose, for no single answer or outlook can repeat its first success and permanently halt mind's movement toward rejuvenation. The second instance already marks a submissive present, a superior past. Regarding such repetitions as a conspiracy against genius, mind must move on, must be a continuum of fixations and dissolutions. As Lawrence

Rosenwald points out when discussing Emerson's journal, even "memory" must be both cumulative and progressive, a process of "incessant purification" (the epithet is Emerson's).[14] Memory is not a passive replaying of images and experiences. Memory recalls the past only to improve on it: "Any piece of knowledge I acquire today . . . has value at this moment exactly proportioned to my skill to deal with it. To-morrow, when I know more, I recall that piece of knowledge and use it better" (*W,* 12:91). Knowing "better than to claim any completeness for my picture" (*CW,* 3:47), Emerson lives to see and feel power incarnate again and again, to remember it, unpredictably, sometimes monstrously, sometimes sweetly. Life is thought in action, memory is past action reactivated in thought, and, when thought and action occur simultaneously, when genius and power come together as one and mind no longer suffers the recriminations of reflection and nostalgia, then will mind gladly endure temporality. Law will give way to will, circumstance to revision, intellection to instinct, for what follows true theory's initiation is "the true romance which the world exists to realize . . . the transformation of genius into practical power" (p. 49).

However, following his own injunction, Emerson does not insist that this is how mind should work, for that would relate any particular exertion of power to the one right exertion and judge it accordingly. It is but one effective possibility, proved to be good today, but it is not necessarily the Good forever. To claim that it is, to posit eternal flux or undivided action as the foundation for progressive thinking, would institute yet another form of correspondence and turn mind's "transformation of genius into practical power" into an ideal form or set procedure. But Emerson's rule of transformation is not a logical proceeding or proper method making the same truth claims that, say, Descartes, Kant, or Husserl make for their respective methods of thinking and of analyzing thought. It is a "romance," a mode of enchanted description belying the rules of realistic representation, the tests of correspondence. The Emersonian conversion of intellect into action, or, better, of reflective thinking into prospective thinking (Emerson does not wish to oppose thought to action—the whole point is to make thought just as active as body is), resists formal stasis, even the stasis of constant conversion.

Transformation itself must be transformed, else it settles into another content, an object of study, a technique to repeat. Unless transformation evolves, unless it always risks an infinite and unforeseeable future, it con-geals into a bit of abstract knowledge, a subject matter to be analyzed, evaluated, and reflected on like any other piece of information. Precisely the reflective break that active Emersonian thinking avoids, the objectifi-cation of mind's dynamic workings turns the course of power back on it-self, perverts "The Natural History of Intellect" into an ever more abstract inwardness. And such solipsistic hebetude has nowhere to go but further into its own ruminations, nothing to do but reify its self-consciousness over and over into a subject matter to ponder. Emerson eschews that vicious circle of self-consciousness. He counsels instead a transition from one circle to another, for "transition is the attitude of power. A fact is only a fulcrum of the spirit. It is the terminus of a past thought, but only a means now to new sallies of the imagination and a new progress of wis-dom" (*W,* 12:59). Of course, thinking absolute "transition" is impossible—it can only be conceived as a principle, not experienced as a concrete referent. Thought must have its fulcra and termini. But if transition can exist only as an abstraction, it remains the only abstraction, the only fixture possessing authority in Emerson's thinking. When it comes to thought's ideal posture, the only principle that Emerson affirms is openness—his only exclusion is exclusion (exclusion being the functional process of any thinking that solidifies, that becomes a set state of mind).[15] "The only sin is limitation" (*CW,* 2:182).

However, this principle serves not to lay the grounds for a liberal plural-ism or general social attitude of toleration. To Emerson, such societies generally betray a failure of their individual members' convictions. If openness or pluralism means that each individual's imaginings have equal value, then such homogenizing formulas serve the herd instinct just as correspondence or tradition presently does and are just as authoritarian. An open society grants to all citizens' visions a generic validity and admits them all accordingly—admits all of them, that is, save one, the vision that violates the principle of acceptance, that posits itself as superior to others and tries to exclude them. Since any original vision implicitly denounces conventional seeing and any superior thinking shames the commonplace understanding, an open society must oust them. But, of course, in so doing, it ensures its own mediocrity.

Emerson's concept of openness is designed specifically to thwart that de-cline. It confers on all visions an equal metaphysical value, a like eligibility to become the "universal sense." But it also acknowledges and does not try to suppress the unequal power backing those visions. That is, Emerson's pluralism accepts the trial of strength carried out as soon as an individual's vision enters the social marketplace as a legitimate criterion of worth. In that manner, Emerson's openness serves to inspire greater and more subversive expressions of practical power—"great men exist that there may be greater men"—which is to say, more insistent exclusions: "every individual strives to grow and exclude and to exclude and grow . . . and to impose the law of its being on every other creature." The openness that Emerson advocates undermines authority ruthlessly but only to institute a new authority, an "amelioration" (*CW,* 4:20, 16, 20) perhaps, but still a powerful closure, one somehow or to someone more liberating and progressive than the old.

To free intellect for divine growth, an inspired visionary must upset the elevated social position of certain kinds or results of power and thereby overcome their stultifying effects. (This stultification results, not from power per se, but from any interpretation of a particular power as not originating in a mind-nature relation.) He or she must attribute the differences between visions to historical or institutional practices, leveling them metaphysically and hence opening them up for revision: "what was yesterday foreground, being today background;—what was surface, playing now not a less effective part as basis" (*W,* 6:64). Stasis sets in when a present "basis" disguises its past "surface," when a former innovation assumes the status of having always been, of being given from the beginning. But givenness signifies, not the truth of nature, but the cowardice of mind. Emerson's lesson is courage of mind, the courage to revise the wisdom of the world, to limit the veritable understanding that made mind what it is (at that moment).

Certain that the guilt of transgressing the order of things testifies to mind's penetration, and likewise assured that imputations of heresy or madness confirm mind's revolutionary course—"Society does not like to have any breath of question blown on the existing order" (*W,* 4:97)—mind can confidently project its own visions and revisions into the arena of conflicting interpretations. Seeing givenness and correspondence as institutional constraints, not natural limits, mind views its visions with a new integrity. With mind now convinced of itself, nature no longer appears as a text to be interpreted faithfully. Nature is now a dormant field of wavering energies or potential doings ready to be attracted and organized, a divine occasion awaiting mind's spiritual exercise. Nature is an active growth, life opening itself to spirit in "whole centrifugal progression," and the best mind can do is to align itself with it.[16] And this alignment need not be passive; mind need not be imposed on by natural force. Instead, mind should meet nature by attraction. Emerson writes (in "Power"), "Perhaps there are men whose magnetisms are of that force to draw material and elemental powers, and, where they appear, immense instrumentalities organize around them" (W, 6:53). The central man or woman is literally a center, a focus around which things come into view. Although "material and elemental powers" precede his or her unconscious administration of them, those powers become available to human being, become instrumental, only after a forceful mind's magnetic orientation. These sublime energies do not act as a prehuman ground of experience; rather, they function as a metaphysical limit demarcating human activity. That is, the "elemental" means nothing except within the context of its humanization, a process that begins with the formation of chaos into locus, a phenomenological mobilization of force initiated once mind realizes its own power.

Because this late retrospective world forbids such pristine beginnings, an original organization must first effect a critical disorganization. Then, to become authentically self-reliant it must detach itself from that negation, for opposition is just an inverted form of influence. One might say, then, that prospective thinking merely ignores its ideological backgrounds and historical-material contingencies. To some politically or sociologically inclined critics, perhaps, Emersonianism is only a strategic presumption of innocence, a naive belief that one can transcend "the wheels of tendency" and "the forces of inertia" (p. 17), a self-reliance fulfilled by reaching beyond history—which is to say, by negating the other's history.[17] That is, Emersonianism is just another intellectual rationalization of conquest. But, although accurate, perhaps, in some political contexts and in a certain diagnostic way, such a judgment is partial and misleading in that it takes one possible political outcome of Emersonian thinking as a necessary result: it posits imperialism and ethnocentrism as the unavoidable strategy of a mind in conflict with history.

But, first of all, an Emersonian mind is not simply antihistorical—that conflict with history implies a kinship with history. Second, if a self-reliant mind obliterates the other's past (presumably to aggrandize its own present), it loses the opportunity to think the other's otherness, to explore the other's world, to expand its own cognitions by recognizing the other's thinking. Our "social strengths" lie in the search not for those like ourselves but rather for those we know not. Emerson writes in *Representative Men,* "Each man seeks those of different quality from his own, and such as are good of their kind; that is, he seeks other men, and *the otherest*" (*CW,* 4:4). Third, this ideological diagnosis removes choice from politics. It denies any variation between epistemology and ethics, says that particular thoughts and particular actions stand in a one-to-one relation. This political interpretation assumes that, if individuals think in a certain way, then they will necessarily act in a certain way, that this thought always yields that act.

In sum, this interpretation of Emerson translates a complex metaphysics of anticorrespondence into a simple politics of appropriation and regards the relation between metaphysics and politics as directly causal. But a particular metaphysical assumption may lead to any one of a variety of political stances, and the latter may not be deduced from the former, for vision is too complex, and there are too many other historical and personal and social variables involved in the activation of vision to make that deduction. Of course, ways of thinking and ways of acting are inextricably connected, but they do not share a necessary connection in all their particulars. And this postulate has Emersonian benefits. It means that mind has not only a choice of vision but also a choice of how to realize that vision in history and society, a choice any visionary must make if he or she is to transform vision into "practical power." This is why Emerson never tries to disguise or to excuse the slide from metaphysics to politics, intellect to action. In fact, his overriding intention is to make that conversion happen and to make it do so as a matter of deliberation, free thinking, an awareness of but not bondage to tradition.

What he laments is precisely the withdrawal of theory from practice, of intellect from action—from ideology, if you will—of mental production from material production. Such a divorce is bound to occur, for example, whenever theory decays into a mere reflection of nature or a hypothesis about nature. Such an abstract manner of theorizing removes itself from nature and denies a natural interest, a human involvement, in its respective motives and outcomes. In contrast to true theory, which reorients mind and nature, abstract theory forgets the original relatedness of mind and nature, mistakenly interpreting the former as individual perceiver and the latter as inert matter. Abstract theory marks a false disinterestedness, a factitious breakdown of "Man Thinking" into "the thinker" and "the thought." These static nominalizations signify the collapse of an active, agonistic dynamic of power and receptivity, Mind and Nature, into a merely circumstantial opposition of discrete entities. The fact that the "possibility of interpretation lies in the identity of the observer with the observed" (*CW,* 4:7) means that theorizing acts on a single but complex identity, not two identities utterly alien to each other coming together through some historical circumstance. There must always already be some categorical connection between them: "Like can only be known by like" (p. 7).

But, in reifying "thinker" and "thought" into distinct and complete things, abstract theory freezes the influxes and strivings that propel the life of the mind. It thereby shadows "Man Thinking" as a settled polarity of subject and object (with the subject no less objectified than its object). But "Man [and Woman] Thinking" is a present progressive, a dialectical rest-lessness out to embrace ever more comprehensive prospects. Thinking does so, however, not to reach either an absolute grasp or a total unity. Rather, thinking strives to grasp the relations bringing differences to-gether, the limiting structures out of which differences emerge. Abstract theorists forget, Emerson writes in "Plato; or, The Philosopher," that "every mental act,—this very perception of identity or oneness, recognizes the differences of things. Oneness and Otherness. It is impossible to speak, or to think without embracing both" (*CW,* 4:29). And, even though one must speak of them nominally or think of them as actually distinct things, to avoid the trap of abstraction one must withstand regarding "Oneness" and "Otherness" as themselves things. They are more, one might say, competing gravitations, each "a huge instrumentality of means" mounting thinker, thought, and nature into "a terrific unity" or circulating them "directly backwards to diversity" (pp. 38, 29, 29; Emerson aligns the unify-ing tendency with "speculation," the diversifying one with "action").

Plato, "the balanced soul" (*CW,* 4:31), synthesizes these "gods of the mind"—both of them necessary to thinking—not, however, to transcend oneness and otherness. Rather, "Plato came to join, and, by contact, to enhance the energy of each," to aggravate the tension of their antithesis. Interested more in energy than solutions, Plato adroitly manages his beliefs across this "union of impossibilities" (p. 31). Firmly convinced that "our strength is transitional, alternating" (p. 31), Plato constantly shuns the myopia of one-vision prophets and the bigotry of systematizers. "Intellectual in his aim," but literary and unsystematic in method, Plato "fluxes" the most hardheaded convictions, uses a "dreadful logic . . . in the pleasantest manner" to turn unexamined certainties into "horrible doubts and confusion" (pp. 42, 41, 41), all in an effort to abide by his knowledgeable ignorance. That parasitical ignorance blunts ordinary knowledge, revealing that each posited result endorses unity *or* diversity and does so by an exclusive attention to one or the other, not to one *and* the other.[18] Platonic thinking brings this epistemological partisanship to an end by recapturing "the observation of identity and diversity" (p. 35), by taking a philosophical stand and fathoming the polarities in this difference.

But how is this thinking to retain the thought of Oneness *and* Otherness, of the difference itself, that ever-unthought relation that can be conceptualized only as some abstract thing being related? How can thinking endure as a swirling agon of pure opposition? Unless thinking objectifies difference, regards difference not as an ineffable ontological relation but as a concrete object *in* relation, thinking mentally decomposes into vertigo. Pondering difference per se, mind forfeits its power, for how can mind act effectively when excogitating on this phantom origin, this indeterminate precondition? While the resulting confusions may help Emerson "unsettle all things" and "simply experiment, an endless seeker with no Past at [his] back" (*CW,* 2:188), they hinder him from organizing a new administration of power and conceiving the world anew. Difference is an epistemological abyss, temporarily serviceable perhaps to skeptical purgings of dead beliefs, but lethal to that critical practice whereby "out of unbeliefs a creed shall be formed" (*CW,* 3:43).[19]

Plato sensed the fecklessness of an unrestricted commitment to difference and indeterminacy, realizing that such a commitment itself would have to be made determinate at some point. Therefore, it would be a strategy both contradictory and impotent. This would mark an internal contradiction, a disabling one, not the fruitful kind of contradiction that Emerson favors as an antidote to foolish consistency. No "creed shall be formed" unless it has positive force, and what gives any creed force is, to Emerson, "the ambition of individualism," the power of mind to institutionalize mind's vision into the world's truth. Although Plato embraces difference, the one *and* the other, a seemingly disabling vacillation or indecision, he circumscribes his transitional thinking by the law of "Platonism." Being a representative man, "Plato would willingly have a Platonism, a known and accurate expression for the world, and it should be accurate. It shall be the world passed through the mind of Plato,—nothing less. . . . He has clapped copyright on the world" (*CW,* 4:77). Plato charms the world, serves humanity as the interpreter of nature, his mind the passageway to truth, so that his interpretations solidify into doctrine. Although a fugitive philosopher, a thinker of elusive differences, Plato nevertheless institutes a definitive practice for pursuing that differential phenomenon. He wills his thinking into "Platonism, a known and accurate expression *for* the world," not of the world. That is, it is an instrumentality of means, a practical construct, not a representational response. Accuracy comes up only in that Platonism accurately pictures the world in the mind of Plato. And what makes that mind accurate is both its "copyright" claim, its decided assertion of authorship, and its reception, the extent to which Plato's auditors become disciples.

This is the philosopher's determination: to extend himself into an ism, to make the world over in his own image—for others. Plato wills his theory of nature into truth, indeed, wills it *as* truth, for the theorizing itself organizes the world into a world, presents it for representation, affirmation, use. What disciples of Plato experience is Platonized nature. This account of philosophical conception contains no pure epistemological moment, no perceptual or intuitive event that could then be held apart from the designs of institutionalization or invoked as the fundamental, disinterested cognition. Knowledge is informed power, a force in effect, not a benign acquisition later implemented to serve power. From its very inception, Platonism, like any discipline, holds fast to its forms and contents, tries to expand its practice into an encyclopedic reference and ensure its repetition.

But every school of thinking, even protean Platonism, has its disciplinary boundaries—not only its obvious political exclusions, but also its subliminal epistemological frameworks beyond which one cannot think. Institutional limits to thinking are themselves functions of the extent to which any cognitive attitude reaches. No thinking comprehends everything, can consciously think Oneness and Otherness simultaneously. Under the strain of absolute knowledge, thinking decomposes, becomes formless and directionless, a countless aberration. Thinking unavoidably classifies and categorizes, does symbolic violence to the unthought, familiarizes it into consumable objects and recognizable concepts. Indeed, the unthought is itself merely the opposite or precedent of thought. To proceed rationally and coherently, even when focusing on itself and not its objects, thinking requires a limit, a horizon of understanding outside of which lies a functional, although forever unaccounted for, beyond.

For Emerson, this outside is Nature, always Nature. Nature is the remainder, the sublime excess exceeding thinking all the time, the other side of the thinking relation. Power is after form, force is after expression, intellect is after fixity—nature eternally antagonizes them and escapes them. Nature is Emerson's negative theology, the provisional beyond that negates all of thinking's enabling negations and exclusions, leaving all other theologies unsatisfactory. Plato institutes an academy where Platonism is the text, where the book of nature is written in a reproducible pedagogy. But no matter: "Unconquered Nature lives on, and forgets him" (*CW*, 4:43). Nature cares not for personalities—it "will not be disposed of" (p. 44) by any individual. Indeed, the greatness of an individual genius lies in his or her capacity to lead others into "an elemental region wherein the individual is lost," where the "thought and feeling that break out there, cannot be impounded by any fence of personality" (p. 18). Thinking follows a process, a conceiving whereby a new idea instantly congeals into a method, a social practice usually associated with the person who conceived it but available for widespread use (and eventually tyrannizing the thinking that produced it, that realized itself within it). Thinking cannot displace nature, only culture. Enlightened thinking first remembers that "our culture is the predominance of an idea which draws after it this train of cities and institutions" and then exhorts others, "Let us rise into another idea: they [cities and institutions] will disappear" (*CW*, 2:179). But, while ideas compete for "predominance," the method of nature surges ahead, blithely indifferent to the social and institutional checks of all humanisms.

But what is nature's method? As Emerson describes it in his occasionally overlooked 1841 address on the subject, "The Method of Nature," nature seems entirely unmethodical. It "does not exist to any one or to any number of particular ends, but to numberless and endless benefit . . . obey[ing] that redundancy or excess of life which in conscious beings we call *ecstasy*" (*CW,* 1:126–27).[20] Nature works by constant exorbitance, a redundancy not like that of doctrine, which asks for arithmetic repetitions, but rather like that of excess, which generates an exponential growth, an excess of excess. Nature is "an ever novel effect," a nascent panorama "in rapid metamorphosis" (pp. 124, 126) meeting the mind's eye. While "conscious beings" have a name for this process—"ecstasy"—they can never wholly join that process without losing a measure of consciousness. They cannot experience that process fully consciously, for to be conscious is to grasp, to hold back, if only for a moment, that becoming display, in the very act of doing so interpreting nature as that which is to be grasped. The problem is, then, how can any attempt to restore thinking back into nature's "metaphysical and eternal spring" avoid thought's inevitable resting place in "the same old vein or crust" (pp. 124–25, 123) of abstraction? How can any theory of nature account for nature's multiplicitous interplay when "that rushing stream will not stop to be observed" (p. 124)? The intellect yields a "crystal sphere of thought," a sclerotic law that "becomes insupportably tedious in a few months," despite our "pulse-beat of expectation," our "invincible hope of a more adequate interpreter" (pp. 122–23). But nature hastens on, unconcerned with the properly worshipful but sometimes vain strivings of intellect. Ever present to mind, or, rather, successively presencing itself to vision, nature is a stern but abiding preceptor, a permanent counterpoise to intelligence. One might affirm a consanguinity of nature and intelligence, but not an identification of them, for the latter is always in a position of trying to hurry up and catch the former. Although nature's permanence is continual and proximate, thinking never entirely apprehends it, for "[nature's] permanence is a perpetual inchoation" (p. 124). The method of nature is a becoming, a ceaseless overcoming, a consort and conflict of Oneness and Otherness, nature at the present and nature in the future. And this movement, drive, impulse, does not end with transcendence, Spirit, Idealism. It never ends, it yields Prospects—it is Life.

Intellect tends to consolidate this fecund transience into a stable theory of nature, one in which mind at once knows itself and finds itself dislocated from and holding back the natural flux. In the despiritualized intellect, nature moves from solution to precipitate, from an animate intermingling of attractions and repulsions to a fossilized "empirical science," an "addition or subtraction or other comparison of known quantities" (*CW,* 1:39), as Emerson puts it in *Nature*. But, no matter how much the "naturalist" "separates and classifies things, endeavoring to reduce the most diverse to one form" (p. 40), nature continues on its peremptory, refulgent course, blithely answerable only to rhapsody, power, and virtue, "paeans of joy and praise" (p. 122; "The Method of Nature"). It allows the naturalist his field of play but derides his pretense, his interpretation of that minor field of uniform objects as representative of the universe at large.

Ordinarily, the Heraclitean language of continuity that Emerson occasionally borrows can rationalize nature's incomprehensible method, can objectify absolute flux into the normative course of events. But, in Emerson's indirect representation of it, nature's method unbounds flux, constitutes nature's process as more than just the regular change of a waterfall. The latter interpretation makes natural processes unified, linear, and steady, easily contained by theory. But here, "the wholeness we admire in the order of the world is the result of infinite distribution" (*CW,* 1:124). Although "its smoothness is the smoothness of the pitch of the cataract," that "smoothness" is merely a simulation of organic continuity, a consequence of quick distribution, for "every natural fact is an emanation, and that from which it emanates is an emanation also, and from every emanation is a new emanation" (p. 124). And that transition from one emanation to the next proceeds, not in an organic continuity, but by an unlimited semiosis: "This refers to that, and that to the next, and the next to the third, and everything refers" (p. 125). Nature is a developing semiotic labyrinth, a referential metamorphosis of this into that. While "[man] pretends to give account of himself to himself" (p. 127), to explain human being, nature quickens and overreaches itself in ecstatic jumps of signification. Can any theory replicate this pure diversity, this endless referentiality? Can any thinking maintain the thought of infinite relations in their irreducible difference and limitless reference and still remain coherent?

Of course, given thinking's tendency toward inertia, toward abstract theory, mind is bound to misrepresent nature's referential drift, but, as we have seen, Emerson dismisses the question of accurate correspondence. If every thought is misrepresentative, then the category *misrepresentation* is meaningless. The predication *misrepresentative* would apply to everything and thereby specify nothing and have no use. Indeed, for Emerson, the characterization of nature as a universal semiosis—"everything refers"— renders nature in itself fundamentally uninteresting. Natural semiosis may goad mind out of its stagnant, crusty intellectualizations of life, but mind remains dissatisfied and disturbed until it finds another, better intellectual resting place. Nonstop emanation is too painful and disempowering. To become attractive, nature must have a frame of reference, a reasonably stable ground or meaning staying the forwardness of natural signs or phenomena. Emerson fully realizes that stability requirement. That basis, a function or a process more than a reality or an entity, he says, is human being: "The universal does not attract us until housed in an individual. . . . The ocean is everywhere the same, but it has no character until seen with the shore or the ship. . . . Confine it by granite rocks, let it wash a shore where wise men dwell, and it is filled with expression" (*CW*, 1:127). Without "individual housing," the universal is flat and featureless, an unbounded tedium, a pacific ocean. Until nature reaches a limit (which only mind can produce), until it suffers differentiation, nature cannot be "filled with expression" and hence cannot satisfy mind's longing to incarnate its thoughts. What makes nature interesting is that it interests mind, that it pulls thinking (often against the individual's will) out of one attitude and into another. Without "character," nature is pure and incomprehensible semiosis, a *physis* without *logos,* a distribution without source or determination.

Such an inconceivable, worldless world victimizes individuals just as much as does the world of reified commodities and abstract intellectualisms. If Emerson commands that thinking duplicate nature's reckless indeterminacy, that, although thinking "houses" nature, it always do so in a mobile home, then Emerson sentences thinking to breakdown. Just as, as B. L. Packer says, "the chief difficulty with Emerson's theory of poetry is not the obsolescence to which it dooms the poem but the intolerable strain to which it subjects the poet,"[21] the problem with his proposal for natural, progressive thinking lies in the ecstasy that it demands of the thinker. It may be true that "the rapt saint is found the only logician" (*CW*, 1:122), but such rhapsodies come all too rarely and not at our bidding. Emerson attests in his essay on Montaigne, "If we compute it in time, we may, in fifty years, have half a dozen reasonable hours" (*CW*, 4:101). But, then, perhaps we could not bear to have more than that, or perhaps society could not afford to have too many rhapsodes. Individuals cannot endure unremittant rhapsody, a total metamorphosis without pause. Given the infrequency of these moments of utter transparency, when minds join with nature's semiotic propagation, they push their translations in determinate, interested, individual directions: "Each individual soul is such, in virtue of its being a power to translate the world into some particular language of its own" (*CW,* 1:128).

This translation *is* thinking, one that maintains its power by perpetuation, for "power ceases in the instant of repose; it resides in the moment of transition from a past to a new state" (*CW,* 2:40). But that perpetuation takes the form of permutation, of change from state to state, from one stability destabilized and reformed into a new and better stability. And the task at hand is not to maintain the content of nature through the soul's various transitions and translations, a maintenance prone to the despair of thinking that every thought is either errant or ephemeral. Rather, the task is to keep thinking productive, to make thinking continuous with nature, theory interactive with experience, treating the noncoincidence of those pairs—continuity and interaction do not mean identity—as the condition of mental development. Each moment of rest should give way to a moment of transition before it decays into an unconscious custom. As long as it is lived mindfully and decisively, not passively rehearsed, a theoretical result or an epistemological rest has force. But also, because "every ultimate fact is only the first of a new series" (p. 181), thinking should be an expanding comprehension, an instrumentality bringing greater and greater worlds to fruition, delivering wider circles to consuming intelligences.

Only by preserving the interests and motives of mental effort at the same time that it clutches for the infinite, only by celebrating the circumstantial contingencies of mind's translations of and rhapsodies on sublimity, can individuals keep their attractions prolific. If an individual soul relinquishes its agency, then certain master translations (prime examples for Emerson would be Christianity and industrial capitalism) become hegemonies, institutionalized thoughts whose condition of origination have been repressed. Instead of remaining the frank, outspoken visions of rival geniuses, translations decay into repetitions, social rituals, bureaucratic decisions. Translation thus becomes an end in itself, despite the fact, Emerson says in "The Method of Nature," that "a man's wisdom is to know that all ends are momentary, that the best end must be superseded by a better. But there is a mischievous tendency in him to transfer his thought from the life to the ends, to quit his agency and rest in his acts: the tools run away with the workman, the human with the divine" (*CW,* 1:129). Mind in power openly acknowledging the contingency of its individuality restores to life the supersession of translations, the human parallel to nature's emanations. Mind thinking an original relation between its historical existence and the extrahistorical nature always beside it awakens society from a state of rest, from a mode of production in which technology assumes the state of nature and individuals become the tools of their tools. Such acts of genius shame any culture in which individuals behave like "some Boswell or listening worshipper to this saint or to that" (p. 129). In attending to the other side of the human—nature, eternity, divinity—but without negating the human—history, culture, individuality—mind alights on the genuine purpose of worship: not a surpassing of self, time, and death through vacant, unconscious reveries of nature as the beyond (a pseudotranscendence), but a thoughtful abandonment of all narrowing conceptions of being and an ecstatic abandonment to nature's excesses. Therein lies mind's unique capacity, its most creative, inspirited moment: "As the power or genius of nature is ecstatic, so must its science or the description of it be" (p. 132).

So true theory interpreted as the thought formulation to answer all questions and satisfy all desires is but the empiricist's version of truth, the conceptual orientation that completes empirical study and beyond which the empiricist cannot see. The scientist believes that such a theory would resolve competing perspectives, reconstituting contrary conclusions into a converging scientific method, with ideology and history falling prey to its universal objective sweep. Then scientific theory would erase its resolution, its simplifying gesture, for, if it did not, it would remain as yet another perspective, a conditional interpretation. But, to the scientist, that theory is not a condition—it is the end of conditioning, the last preparation for solid empirical description. An ultimate deciphering, it finalizes the history of intellect and readies the way for pure unbiased observation, breaking the code of nature's semiotic and finally allowing for an unmitigated, unvitiated calculation and classification of things.

Emerson likewise regards true theory as the completion of scientific thinking. But, while the scientist honors true theory as the extremity of knowledge bringing the dense, casual world of matter and energy to transparency, Emerson considers it a graduation, a revelatory transition pitching mind toward apprehensions of life exceeding that theory's coverage.

What the scientist experiences as the decisive perception Emerson experiences as one possible apperception. True theory is the whole truth of scientific thinking (here aligned with empiricism), but true theory to Emersonian thinking is the truth of the whole world to which scientific thinking applies itself. That is, arriving at true theory, the total explanation of phenomena, a spirited mind recognizes the phenomenal world as a whole, thereby cognizing an other world as well. And, if it is the case that "the feeling of the world as a limited whole is the mystical feeling,"[22] then the act of rendering whole that existence that previous thinking was wholly captivated by is the supreme act of thinking. It is the closing of one circle to feel one's way mystically (Emerson would prefer the term *worshipfully*) to another region of being, knowing of course that captivation is part of getting to know that world elsewhere. But what determines mind's act of "wholing" one world and envisioning another is not so much a consequence of truth or theory or even worship. Although the allotment of conscious choice that mind enjoys on its intellectual journey is often, Emerson implies, rather negligible, at these spiritual encounters, at each unsettling concourse of universes, mind can still resolve what to make of it and what to do with it. And deciding what counts as worship, which truths and theories have the most explanatory value, is a question not of mysticism but of pragmatism.

Chapter Two

William James's Psychology
of Pragmatic Thinking

Brooding on the patriotic backlash that his *Hawthorne* evoked from American critics, specifically his highlighting the "crude and simple society in which [Hawthorne] lived,"[1] Henry James repeatedly takes occasion to assert the parochial thinness of American culture. He regards Americans' defensive accusations that he had over-Anglicized himself merely as further evidence of the vulgar provincialism of American life: "The whole episode [of hostile reviews and notices of *Hawthorne*] projects a lurid light upon the state of American 'culture,' and furnishes me with a hundred wonderful examples, where, before, I had only more or less vague impressions."[2] Indeed, given that "in the United States, in those days [Hawthorne's time], there were no great things to look at (save forests and rivers); life was not in the least spectacular; society was not brilliant; the country was given up to a great material prosperity, a homely *bourgeois* activity, a diffusion of primary education and the common luxuries,"[3] it is miraculous that a novelist of Hawthorne's caliber ever emerged. James notes that even Hawthorne himself had lamented in his preface to *The Marble Faun* "the difficulty of writing a Romance about a country where there is no shadow, no antiquity, no mystery, no picturesque and gloomy wrong, nor anything but a common-place prosperity, in broad and simple daylight, as is happily the case with my dear native land"[4] (this drawback William Dean Howells considered as further testimony to Hawthorne's genius). This is why, in analyzing Hawthorne's corpus, James often returns to what he considers the fundamental interest in Hawthorne's situation: "The beauty of Hawthorne's genius in comparison with the provinciality of his training and circumstances."[5]

James's conclusion that the defects of Hawthorne's writings rest in the bare milieu he chose to fictionalize would seem to evince James's disdain for his homeland, his assumption that only by leaving America could he flower into a great artist. The American scene is simply too blank and immature, too ahistorical, to offer the novelist a fitting climate of representation, for "it takes a great deal of history to produce a little literature." The New World milieu may suit the Emersonian sage, whose "doctrine of the supremacy of the individual . . . must have had a great charm for people living in a society in which introspection, thanks to the want of other entertainment, played almost the part of a social resource."[6] (Obviously, the Emersonianism that James has in mind differs from that of the previous chapter.) But, to the Jamesian novelist searching for the sense and sensations of others' lives, America is a homogeneous society of common, conforming, present-minded individuals who see others and themselves only as objects. Their introspection is not a celebration of self but rather a pathetic recourse to inwardness to compensate for the sparse particulars of American society and the inhuman immensities of the continent, leaving "each citizen," Tocqueville writes, "habitually engaged in the contemplation of a very puny object: namely, himself."[7] The self-centered poetorator may pretend or even believe that America is a virgin landscape open to heretofore repressed human energies. But his or her dream of selfdiscovery is really a disguised consolation, a symptom of cultural ennui, a pitiful Whit-mania, James might say.[8] For the Jamesian writer, America remains a kindergarten, a materialistic playground without gods or a past to dignify Americans' innocence or hubris.

But, although James does condemn culture in America throughout his life, he does not always or so unambiguously dismiss an American's experience of culture. Indeed, in the majority of James's fiction, the complexity of that experience fuels the plot and narration (even though the Ameri-

can's experience often proves to be ultimately disappointing), a fact indicating the dramatic opportunities and satisfactions that James discovered in
staging Americans abroad. Also, one could cite several statements outside
the fiction that indicate directly James's ambivalent feelings about America: for example, Hamlin Garland's testimony that James once said to him
late in life, "If I were to live over again, I would be an American. I would
steep myself in America. . . . I would study its beautiful side."[9] A more
critical, less personal opinion appears in a well-known letter to his close
friend Thomas Sergeant Perry (dated 20 September 1867), one worth
quoting extensively. Here, a young Henry James, already settled on a
literary career, turns the impoverished state of American culture into a
surprising privilege for those growing up in it:

> We are Americans born—*il faut prendre son parti*. I look upon it as a
> great blessing and I think that to be an American, is an excellent prepa-
> ration for culture. We have exquisite qualities as a race, and it seems to
> me that we are ahead of the European races in the fact that more than
> either of them we can deal freely with forms of civilization not our own,
> can choose and assimilate, and in short, aesthetically, etc., claim our
> property where we find it. To have no national stamp has hitherto been
> a regret and a drawback, but I think it not unlikely that American
> writers may yet indicate that a vast intellectual fusion and synthesis of
> various national tendencies of the world is the condition of more im-
> portant achievements than any we have seen.[10]

Cited by Horace Kallen as a perfect instance of the "American Idea,"[11] this
patriotic summation of American prospects explains James's constant ex-
patriation: to realize one's Americanness, one must search out "forms of
civilization *not our own*" and "fuse" and "synthesize" them into a vision of
future "achievements." Rather than rebelling against the (European) past
by casting it as an obsolete feudal mistake or preserving one's innocence or
ignorance through a commitment to nature, Americans must meet other
cultures and their pasts and incorporate them, use them as an opportunity
for growth, for what is not our own is the precondition of American
expansion, the necessary otherness that Americans overcome in order to
supersede the past and transcend their present selves. Hence, the Hegelian
language of fusion and synthesis, a language that does away with simple
oppositions of nature and culture, past and future, East and West. Re-

nouncing the Emersonian consignment of the past to oblivion, James characterizes his sojourn through Europe as the American dream in reverse. Instead of sauntering off into the naked continent and building a world elsewhere, he returns eastward, composing himself into a conglomerate of foreign traditions, a sponge soaking up "various national tendencies of the world" and translating them into a New World understanding.

In both versions—we might call them the Adamic and the Jamesian[12]—Americans "assimilate" and "claim . . . property" as "ours." However, in the former myth, Americans reclaim "original energy" and domesticate a wilderness, while in the latter they appropriate a national culture, not simply by buying its artifacts and aristocrats, but by applying to them a pre- or supranational awareness. They will succeed so well, he predicts, precisely because they have no culture of their own, "no national stamp," and so can "deal freely" with national differences, be receptive to the other's heritage and uninhibited by the propriety accompanying it. Their minds not limited by any filial perspective, Americans enjoy a rare structural privilege over those borne into a nationalized time and place. While the Frenchman, Florentine, or Egyptian must regard national and ancestral borders as the condition of self-preservation, Americans treat geographic and historical differences with indifference, recognizing the border as something to cross, to absorb. And this moment of overcoming is not just a political act of appropriation—it is the Americans' act of self-recognition. Expansion is how they find themselves. They have "no national stamp," so they must stamp themselves "internationally."

In fact, apart from a vague attachment to abstractions such as *freedom* and *equality,* and despite their hostility to anything un-American, Americans (in James's interpretation) have no political or cultural commitments to America itself. They do not adhere to America without opposing its other, for there is no pure America. Neither a nationality, nor a history, nor really a place, America is the *act* of confronting and overcoming Europe, one that must face a European thesis before it can come into its own. America is a geopolitical process, not a natural identity. It is a strategy of assimilation out to realize itself by surpassing (but not blindly negating) its precursors. To James, Adamic America is simply a communal repression, an attempt to forget the thing that identifies Americans: their difference from the Old World. The Adamic myth involves escaping such differences and confrontations entirely, doing so under the guise of a recuperation of nature.

In fact, notwithstanding those sublime descriptions of primal moments of seeing and being in Emerson, Whitman, et al., Adamism stages simply a muddled impulse facing a natural vacancy, a subjective desire wanting to materialize its life in an atmosphere of natural depth and moral rightness but floundering on a blank objective surface.

Such prospects prove to be inadequate for James and his characters. One brief example is from *The American:* Christopher Newman explaining why he has come to Paris. A few months earlier, he says, waiting in a hack outside the stock market, just about to take a half-million-dollar revenge on a competitor, he suddenly finds himself disgusted with his Wall Street practices. Tired and contemptuous of a lifetime of material gain, realizing that the American self-made man's self-making amounted merely to "add[ing] dollars to dollars," Newman renounces "the whole proposition" and reclines in his hack like a "corpse." As he does so, he dimly feels a revivifying force starting to life within him, but the society he presently inhabits only suppresses him: "I seemed to feel a new man under my old skin; at all events I longed for a new world." Stripped of his commercial ambitions, seeing no other activity that might reinvigorate his spirit, Newman seems ripe for an Adamic regeneration. Yet a jaunt across Brooklyn ferry (à la Whitman), a drive out into the country, and a morning spent "looking at the first green leaves on Long Island" provide no comfort or direction for his life, each country escape leaving him just as vexed and dissatisfied as before. These predictable Adamic retreats do not answer "his strong yearning, a desire to stretch out and haul in." He craves a different landscape, one not empty of culture but full of history, one that will not be so easily claimed. Meandering in nature to absorb its innocent splendors does not alter Newman's condition, for nature and the stock market call for the same ahistorical grasping speculation. Because American nature (and culture) seems only too open for quick consumption, Newman concludes that his only satisfaction, the real "new world," lies in the Old World: "As soon as I could get out of harness I sailed for Europe."[13]

Newman's parable illustrates the plight that Americans endure if they insist on their exceptionalism, if they interpret their global difference as a rupture instead of as a relation. Severed from instead of defined against their past, Americans are culturally empty. James does refer a few lines further in his letter to Perry to "something of our own . . . our moral consciousness, our unprecedented spiritual lightness and vigor."[14] But, although they are "exquisite qualities," such features are motives for action, not reflection. They neither compose an identity nor store up historical content. Rather, they are forces of acquisition, natural drives to know and to possess: "vigor" ceaselessly propels Americans, "lightness" commits them to no single project save projection. And American "moral consciousness," supporting projection with simplistic justifications, enables Americans to move on to further growth without deliberating over the meaning or memory of past expansions.

This is what makes Americanization such an "excellent preparation for culture," what makes inessentiality an advantage, not a drawback (as long as Americans are properly adjusted to their dialectical condition). Because they realize themselves by progressive assimilations of the other, Americans form no lasting connections between personal experience and national institutions, between private interest and the body politic. They owe no allegiances to what they relinquish or what they find, so their flights and foundings can take the form of a clean break, an innocent discovery. With nothing of themselves personally at stake in operations of culture and history, they retain their ingenuousness, their ignorance of any other motive but expansion. Always directed toward a future synthesis, they remain relatively undetermined by any established history of what they wish to grow into. Even though this political dexterity sometimes assumes the form of a mythical prepolitics, a grounding in nature, and in the eyes of many critics proves to be a basic imperialist maneuver, it has astonishing political force. Careless of evaluating their experiences by the yardstick of tradition, unconcerned with accommodating themselves to any genealogical demands, Americans can choose and assimilate with the dispatch and security of fearless children. And, to repeat, their actions stem from a mental condition, not a political decision. Although the former has immediate political effects, James's abstract geopolitical language signifies, not a politics of travel, but an epistemology of international awareness. The question is, how can Americans move from epistemology to action, from the mental "preparation for culture" to the process of "acculturation," without endangering their mental freedom, without sinking themselves too much in others' history?

To organize their arrogations innocently, Americans require only a congenial method, a practice as pure and American as their guileless, grasping sensibilities. If that method has an interest attached to it and hence a content that it must sustain, a direction that it is predisposed to take, then it will compromise its wielder's neutrality and candor. If it has a limited application, then it will disappoint the limitless scope expected of an American vision. Also, as it engages mind with history, culture, or nationality, it threatens to commit mind to or ground mind in some particular historical moment—the very antithesis of Americanness. To avoid these pitfalls, Americans must develop a method of expanding comprehensions, one that will keep up with the dialectical restlessness of the American mind. Since Americans find themselves through actions of assimilation, the action itself must somehow coincide with them—mind and method must coalesce so that they come into being together in every moment of assimilation. If they do not, then, although an other may be assimilated, the means of assimilation itself remains artificial and impersonal, a factitious technique, and every American's act of self-discovery by assimilation risks self-alienation. If this essential action becomes reified into a set technique, then the method becomes just as limiting and static as the particular historical-cultural content mind supposedly transcends in that act. To avoid that formal pitfall, American action must be a method simultaneous with mind, constantly in process, reflecting mind's self-revisions, American by virtue of its tendency toward no permanent national or political end.

Henry James provides us with a brief model of one kind of American mind, a portrait of sensibility primed for global achievements. One might consider his theory of expatriate experience a geopolitical analogue to Emerson's program of mental world building. James's crisp formulation connects American mind to international experience, forecasts method, migrant politics, and the American mind as the terms in which the future of Western civilization will be decided. But, in his plots, that mind usually ends up as a passive observer-victim whose American presumptiveness is treated ironically or tragically. One might say that his most American characters fail to discover a workable method, one that would immerse them in other cultures yet preserve them as transcultural, free and active despite their circumstances. This is virtually the same criticism that William James leveled at Henry himself, or at his literary methods: that in his later novels he employed a "method of narration by interminable elaboration of suggestive reference," getting so caught up in depicting with brilliance and clarity a "high-toned social atmosphere" that his narratives lack any "great vigor and decisiveness in the action."[15] According to William, when Henry applied his method, in this case, to turn-of-the-century European upper-crust society, he became lost in its minute discriminations, enervated by its mannered subtleties. Method was seduced by subject matter, the American artist subsumed by his foreign material. The great American synthesis did not follow, and, instead of transcending European culture, Henry found himself endlessly involved in enumerating its workings.

William eschews this kind of abnormal activity, as he described Henry's writing, preferring the vigorous thinking that he describes and develops in his own writings. Although not as concerned with American issues as is his younger brother, William is fairly obsessed with the mental traits characterizing Henry's American *cogito:* prospection, assimilation, transhistoricity. He dedicates his researches to advancing philosophies that maintain mind's processual character, that keep mind from crystallizing into a mental substance or becoming grounded in a physical substance. In practical terms, one might say that he seeks a psychic method ever ready to disengage from subject matter, a method satisfying Henry's sociocultural fusion but not becoming overly socialized or acculturated in one spot. For William, the most effective strategy for free mental action is, of course, pragmatism. Or, rather, the pragmatic method, for pragmatism is an action, not a theory, a mode of thinking, not a philosophy—it instrumentalizes all intellectual concepts and abstractions: "Pragmatism unstiffens all our theories, limbers them up and sets each one at work." What makes pragmatism so effective is that it has no policies to represent, no ideas to espouse, no interests to promote except those of satisfaction. It promises to be as transpolitical as Henry's American mind, inclined to submit any historical and political content to the latter's unrestricted, evolving assimilations. Bearing no content in itself, no predetermined answers or solutions, it maintains an ideological agility through time, a thoroughgoing openness to whatever future result may be in order. "It is a method only," James writes, a "program" that "stands for no particular results" and that "has no dogmas, and no doctrines save its method." A simple and simplifying activity, pragmatism's sole initial requirement is "an attitude of orientation": "*The attitude of looking away from first things, principles, 'categories,' supposed necessities; and of looking toward last things, fruits, consequences, facts.*"[16]

One could treat this attitude as a moral adjustment in the way American thinkers philosophize, whereby "the ethical and political imperative embodied in pragmatism" demands that we "become responsive to and maybe responsible for the future of a belief."[17] An ethical reading of pragmatism would single out its futural orientation, its disregard for any destined particular results. Politically open, although not apolitical, risking disagreement with yesterday's results, pragmatism grants American thinkers a new responsibility for their beliefs and frees them to choose alternatives. When James finally claims that *"the true is the name of whatever proves itself to be good in the way of belief"* (*Pragmatism,* 42), he relocates truth in moral benefit, in a principle of expedience that paves the way for liberal reform and social tolerance. "It appears less as a solution, then, than as a program for more work, and more particularly as an indication of the ways in which existing realities may be *changed*" (p. 32).

But, while the ethical implications of pragmatism may, to James, confirm pragmatism's superiority to rationalism, idealism, monism, and so on, the success of any single implementation of its method rests not on the community service that it provides but on the mental satisfaction that it yields to an individual. Just as Henry's American's political synthesis rests on a certain mental capacity (the absence of a national memory), so William's pragmatism's moral outlook needs psychological backing. Specifically, to James, the cash-value of any method or belief, pragmatism included, lies in the extent to which it converts "inward trouble" to subjective ease. "Inward trouble" being caused by any "new experience" that "puts [old opinions] to a strain" (*Pragmatism,* 34), what is *good in the way of belief"* is whatever "gratifies the individual's desire to assimilate the novel in his experiences to his beliefs in stock" (p. 36). If mind can "admit the novelty" with "a minimum of disturbance," if it can "marr[y] old opinion to new fact so as ever to show a minimum of jolt, a maximum of continuity" (p. 35), then life can continue in an unobstructed "stream of thought." What is good is whatever provides for cognitive relaxation, thought moving smoothly from one experience to the next. This is why James's descriptions of pragmatism at work usually portray it operating through minds, not on society or philosophy as a whole.[18] He relates ideas and beliefs, even those held by a community, to "individual desire," "subjective reasons," and "temperament," implying that what is ethically good must first of all be psychologically good. So, before raising moral and polit-ical questions, James explores forms of mental effectiveness, pursues a use-ful description of cognition and an accompanying outline for satisfaction.

While both brothers pose the question of assimilative thinking, Henry does so by drawing portraits of Americans traversing and faltering over historical and political boundaries, William by scrupulously tracing a tor-tuous clinical excursion through the normal and aberrant workings of the mind from its rawest experiences to its most abstract comprehensions. Like Henry's letters and essays on the American character, William's pre-*Pragmatism* psychological writings (of the 1880s and 1890s) import more than a description of mind at work. They also bear a prescription for right thinking, for effective mental growth, a strategy American not in a histor-ical sense but in a pragmatic sense: the *act* of assimilating the foreign smoothly, of incorporating novel phenomena into a productive, evolving world synthesis. For William, this drama of mind's success and failure really takes place, not in Gilbert Osmond's villa, or in Adam Verver's American city, but rather in the psyche. The future of an individual mind's growth, indeed, all the political and historical manifestations and outcomes of Henry's American prospection, rests on how a mind perceives different colors, when it feels pain, what it thinks a thing is, whether it can endure mystery, how it apprehends its own death, and so on.

At first sight, it might seem that James's definition of pragmatic truth as whatever ideas help us *"get into satisfactory relations with other parts of our experience"* (*Pragmatism,* 34) invalidly joins two distinct subjective acts, that it confuses satisfaction and cognition. Common sense asserts that satisfac-tion is an aftereffect of cognition, strictly a concomitant of percepts and concepts. In that case, pragmatism vainly seeks to submit given sensations and rational ideas to subjective interests. But, for James, cognition is a function of subjective interests, even at the brute level of sensation. In the early essay "Spencer's Definition of Mind," he writes, "These interests are the real *a priori* element in cognition." Because many objects that we encounter in sensation are sometimes "accented with pleasure [or] with pain," our experiences are ordered as follows: "That the pleasant or inter-esting items are singled out, dwelt upon, developed into their farther connections, whilst the unpleasant or insipid ones are ignored or sup-pressed. The future of the Mind's development is thus mapped out in advance by the way in which the lines of pleasure and pain run. The interests precede the outer relations noticed" (*Essays in Philosophy,* 12).[19] This is not a willful, conscious pursuit of pleasure but rather the preconscious standpoint that moves our thinking. A teleology of attention, it precedes mind's "notice." Mind develops through this unconscious arbitration of pleasure and pain and hence cannot assume any position beyond it from which to comprehend it. The only things that we can consciously comprehend are those that the interests of pleasure and pain have prepared for us and compelled us to attend to, never the interests themselves. The only things that we recognize as real, as true, are those that grasp us, that claim our observance: "The only objective criterion of reality is coerciveness" (p. 21).

Used skillfully, the pragmatic method converts this coercive attachment into an affinity between mind and fact, a satisfying relation of ideas, for mind need not sit passively registering sensations. If it adopts an inert, acquiescent attitude, it does so by choice because it is interested in doing so (although this interest need not always be conscious). Coercion may smack of determinism, but, because "mental interests, hypotheses, postulates . . . help to *make* the truth which they declare," "there belongs to mind, from its birth upward, a spontaneity, a vote" (*Essays in Philosophy,* 21). Mind's "judgments of the *should-be,* its ideals, cannot be peeled off from the body of the *cogitandum* as if they were excrescences," for cognition happens only after it has passed through mind's precognitive selective interest.

Mind's teleology, then, is to maintain "lines of pleasure" in the face of developing experiences, to ensure smooth transitions from one experience to the next. However, satisfaction does not spring from the subjective stream itself—only a consciousness can feel satisfaction. A pure stream of consciousness, a mind experiencing sensations, perceptions, and conceptions in continuous and indiscriminate succession, has no coherence, makes no selections, and hence does not constitute thinking: "Without selective interest . . . the consciousness of every creature would be a gray chaotic indiscriminateness, impossible for us even to conceive." As he defines it in *The Principles of Psychology,* consciousness is a whole—not an addition of thoughts, but a totality of thinking, thoughts "all-belonging-together" (381, 220). More than the sum of its parts, consciousness is an organization of Nature's "indistinguishable swarming *continuum,*" a mobilization of interests so pervasive that even "simple sensations are results of discriminative attention" (pp. 274, 219). A sensuous continuum drifts aimlessly along in a "river of elementary feeling" (p. 227), exercising its selective interest only at the passive level of physiology, for example, hearing only those sound waves that ears can hear.

If such a continuum were to exist, mind would not, nor would satisfaction ever occur. For mind to exist, for it to make discriminations, it must have something to discriminate against, some opposition, resistance, impediment, or otherness to assimilate or overleap. Therefore, if mind's teleology is to streamline its pleasures, to determine its next experiences as fully coextensive with its previous ones, then it aims in effect to annihilate itself. If, James writes in "The Sentiment of Rationality," "any unobstructed tendency to action discharges itself without the production of much cogitative accompaniment, and any perfectly fluent course of thought awakens but little feeling" (*Essays in Philosophy*, 33), then the more we "gravitate towards the attainment of such fluency," the more our consciousness disintegrates. Consciousness is inversely proportional to "fluency" and "unobstruction": "When enjoying plenary freedom to energize in the way of motion or of thought, we are in a sort of anaesthetic state."

But this achieved anaesthesia never lasts very long, for mind's self-directed incognizance cannot sustain itself. Mind's tendency to "formulate rationally a tangled mass of fact," to sift all "mutually obstructed elements" into "some new mode of formulation" that provides "mental ease and freedom," inevitably stalls. It blocks itself, and not only for empirical reasons—say, the inexorable onset of a new "tangle"—but by reason of an inherent contradiction in mind's method. Put simply, by postulating an end, even an end that brings about its own end, mind defers that end. The postulated end here would be to stop mind's own postulations, to achieve seamless continuity of experience, openness to the river of life. But, as soon as mind proposes a goal, it lifts experience out of this continuous present, weighs successive subjective moments against a desired future. Giving itself a direction, mind must limit and guide the stream, and in so doing it casts the majority of its experiences as distractions, resistances, deviations, the very things necessitating mindfulness. Once mind sights an end, it must manage its experiences accordingly, thereby becoming directed instead of drifting. No longer a simple sentiment basking in the sufficiency of the present moment, mind is now a projection, inhabiting or rather anticipating a future ever about to be.

Hence, mind reaches an existential impasse. Even though its most fundamental interest is to become disinterested, entirely purposiveless, such a goal is still a conclusion and therefore obeys what might be called James's "law of conclusion": "*For the important thing about a train of thought is its conclusion*. . . . Usually this conclusion is a word or phrase or particular image, or practical attitude or resolve. . . . In either case it stands out from the other segments of the stream by reason of the peculiar interest attaching to it. This interest *arrests* it, makes a sort of crisis of it when it comes, induces attention upon it and makes us treat it in a substantive way" (*Principles,* 251). To "treat [something] in a substantive way" is to substantiate it, to make it stand out and stand still as a something in some way opposed to mind but ready for mental consumption. A peculiar interest attaches to it, making it an it, a discrete object, and setting off a psychological crisis that, as we have seen, makes mind mindful. Any conclusion, even a conclusion of utter inconclusiveness, awakens mind, reverses mind's ostensible goal. Constituting mind and thing together as and in a suspenseful critical arrest, interest induces attention, attention being not simply a willful focus of concentration but the shape and shaping of experience.[20] Even when mind attends to its opposite—"inattentiveness"—it objectifies the latter, cathects it, treats it as some thing to experience. So mind (as mind) can never attain a condition of streamy disinterestedness. Although, James writes, "Thought is in Constant Change" and "*there is no proof that the same bodily sensation is ever got by us twice,*" experience does contain a fundamental repetition that belies pure streaminess: "*What is got twice is the same OBJECT*" (*Principles,* 224–25). Because mind can only attach to things as objects, mind can never wholly join the current. It must always, to some extent, resist it.

In other words, in pursuing a perfect stream and, consequently, its own reduction, consciousness only ensures its survival. Mind applies a self-defeating strategy. The only way for it to work would be if, in setting up this pure stream of becoming as a desired state of being—an act Nietzsche singles out as the "supreme will to power"[21]—mind reaches an absolute conclusion, a site of ultimate discharge that, if not leading to mind's outright demise, does afford mind a calm nirvanic continuity of thinking. This instrument of utter satisfaction—in "The Sentiment of Rationality" James calls it a "metaphysical Datum"—would extend "men's thoughtless incurious acceptance of whatever happens to harmonize with their subjective ends" (*Essays in Philosophy,* 34) to infinity, for now the subject would accommodate all experiences smoothly, fluently, as simple influxes. The conditions of its existence abated, mind would emerge out of its final arrest immersed in immediate experience, achieving "perfectly unimpeded mental function," the equivalence, to James, of absolute rationality (p. 64). And, to repeat, total rationality, a comprehensive explanation of things, cancels itself out: "A unique datum which left nothing else outstanding would leave no play for further rational demand, and might thus be said to quench that demand or to be rational *in se.* No *otherness* being left to annoy the mind we would sit down at peace" (p. 57).

This unique datum provides a uniform, blissful peace precisely because, in rationalizing absolutely, it leaves nothing else to rationalize, nothing outstanding to account for. It is the special truth, instrument, or object that converts all possible disruptive, upsetting encounters into familiar objects and assimilatable experiences, thereby annulling mind's raison d'être. Under the datum's explanatory power, that condition of annoyance—"otherness"—the thing that compelled mindfulness, has given way. Now we may live without the worry that every jolt causes us, the inward troubles that demand that we rationalize our existence. Life's moments become sufficient unto themselves, not rational in themselves, but providing a sentiment of rationality for us, a feeling of relief and contentment that need not be explained or justified.[22]

But mind never reaches a final conclusion—such hope is untenable. First, it forecasts some ideal object that relieves absolutely, one unique datum resolving all past, present, and future data but not itself requiring any resolution. While this object or truth facilitates mind's progressive assimilations, mind cannot and should not assimilate it. Second, and more important, this strategy assumes that annoyance has an object, otherness, which supposedly is out there waiting to be assimilated. But otherness is not an object. Foreign objects may possess some "other" qualities, but otherness is precisely that which stands over and against any object, that which haunts the outside of any objectification. It is not an analogous being but the other of being, not simply nonbeing (which falls easily into the category of absent being) but a bare other irreducible to ontological categories. Because those categories judge otherness only as an other space or an other time, not properly as space's or time's other, ontology can never name the other, never apprehend it as such. But, then, neither can we

borrow the language of epistemology and properly call otherness a nou-
menal idea, a "mere being of thought" (Kant), for it is the other of
thought, not an other thought. It is the unthinkable, for we can think only
what can become an object of cognition. Hence, we have no adequate
means of asking the question, What is the being of otherness? Neither
substance nor meaning nor intention, although our grammar compels us
to articulate it so, otherness will not submit to an ontology of presence-
absence or an epistemology of noumena-phenomena. Between any datum
and otherness lies utter irrelativity.

This means that there is no way to think otherness smoothly (a more
important problem to James than any ontological problem). No philosophy of otherness is possible, is able to appropriate otherness and render it as
object, for mind's methods inevitably hinder its appropriation of otherness. Specifically, were otherness ever convertible into just another alternative datum, something mind could perceive and recognize, mind would
have no play of rationality, no room for mind to work its attachments.
There would be no room for mind. Mind's task is to develop fluid rela-
tivities, to domesticate otherness by forecasting it as yet-to-be-assimilated
data. But a world made up entirely of objects, a world without otherness,
would be already determined, fully cathected, fixed and complete—in a
word, mindless. How could mind function in such a world? Experience
would involve the simple addition of data to mind's inventory, an activity
calling for little attentiveness.[23] With every experiential possibility already
substantiated as a thing, mind's intentionality would be logically set—the
only changes that mind would experience would involve changes of sensuous content.

This satisfying elimination of otherness and connection with things
may ostensibly be mind's *telos,* but mind itself may never occupy such a
world, for otherness is mind's precondition, and every attempt to eradicate
otherness absolutely only brings about the opposite of its own end. Although "*all* that is experienced is, strictly considered, *objective*" (*Principles,*
290), experience can arise only against a backdrop of the inexperienceable,
the latter being an inescapable side effect of any objectification. Indeed,
empirical evidence itself shows that, while always pursuing more universality and extensiveness with every progressive philosophical conception,
mind preserves that which prevents any absolute extension, any totalized
experience. James writes in "The Sentiment of Rationality": "It is an

empirical fact that the mind is so wedded to the process of seeing an *other* beside every item of its experience, that when the notion of an absolute datum which is all is presented to it, it goes through its usual procedure and remains *pointing* at the void beyond, as if in that lay further matter for contemplation" (p. 58). No datum can ever be absolute. Every experience has a concomitant beyond, a coincident not experienced. Even the entirety of existence, the universe, has its other, the void, the latter ever coercing but evading mind's attention. And, no matter how much mind tries to point out and delimit the void, otherness inevitably arises as the by-product of any delimitation. Whether mind's wedded-ness is a structural necessity or an empirical habit, an essential working of thought or merely thought's latent desire, it destines mind to endless negotiations with otherness. In other words, mind's tendencies compel it to treat the void as a "the," some thing to apply the definite article to, knowing that every such treatment is inadequate, that mind should try to constitute the void as a function, not a reality, to experience it as a "beyond" effect, not a present object. The more we try to delineate it, the more we realize that "void" is a pseudonym, a noun deluding us into thinking that the void is another datum. But, in truth, "there is no logical identity, no natural bridge between nonentity and this particular datum" (p. 58).

The void is not another datum, for mind's pointing does not issue in an experience of a present object but rather provides "further matter for contemplation." And, although applied to some matter, contemplation does not simply apprehend it, grasp it as object. *Contemplation* here signifies something closer to its etymological meaning: *con-* (together) + *templum* (a space marked out for divination). It differs from perception in that perception integrates a present sensation and similar past sensations that it revives into a definite object, the whole activity being entirely empirical (see *Principles,* 722–27). Contemplation, on the other hand, involves organizing a place where every perception becomes a metaphysical quest. Such a quest remains contemplative by *not* applying objectifying predicates to the other, by not letting otherness materialize into a mere negation of what is there, into a not there or a not now. A negation of objects shares the same structure as an instantiation of objects, but contemplation eschews such oppositions (and the hope that they bear of the other eventually coming to presence, of the negation being negated). Instead, contemplation minds otherness and data in a tense difference, where one is the alterity of the other. Resisting the natural attitude, contemplation takes the singularity of the thing as a result of forgetting this constitutive alterity, an outcome that uncontemplative thinkers misinterpret as the base of all experience. It holds to its metaphysical awareness precisely by resisting the temptation to treat the object as all or even as first.

However, this does not mean that contemplation merely reverses the empiricist tendency to objectify. Instead of turning around and positing the beyond as all or as the locus of truth—a mystical assertion that James would have rejected, despite his investment in the viability of mystical experience—a contemplative mind preserves both the object and the beyond other, regarding them as functional differences, each one identifying the other. Or, rather, because mind can think the other only as an identity, it maintains its contemplative standpoint by observing strictly the metaphysical difference that brings otherness to thought. Contemplation remains mindful of a differential effect that itself can never be substantiated. If mind were to do otherwise, mind would think empirically only, meditating not an agon of object and other but a pairing of present object and absent object. Realizing that there is always "a possible Other than the actual" (*Essays in Philosophy*, 59), that otherness is the opposite of actuality and vice versa, mind finds that every identification that it makes throws mind back on this object-other difference. And, although mind might be able to articulate the object and the other, at least as concepts, the difference between them will not be identified, cannot even be thought except in the object-other terms that it yields. Mind feels its effects but can never point to it as there. The most that mind can know is that "there is a *plus ultra* beyond all we know, a womb of unimagined other possibility" (p. 59).

But does a metaphysical limit to cognition restrict the directions and uses of cognition? Does the fact that "the notions of a Nonentity . . . still haunt our imagination and prey upon the ultimate data of our system" (*Essays in Philosophy*, p. 59) mean that our contemplations can never progress, that despair is our only legitimate feeling?[24] Obviously, if mind purposes to appropriate Nonentity absolutely, to overcome the object-other limit so that there is no more beyond, then mind condemns itself to dissatisfaction. But, if mind recognizes Nonentity (without attempting to objectify it as a mere emptiness), then a startling adjustment may take place. That is, just because Nonentity never changes—change can be understood only in terms of categories that otherness is beyond—does not mean that mind's relation to it and experience of it may never change. The being (or antibeing) of Nonentity may be immutable (because it has no substance to mutate), but the meaning of this other can be other and better than previously thought. Specifically, James argues, it is a not so difficult step to convert Nonentity from being a paralyzing annoyance to a satisfying cognitive instrument, to accept it as other yet let it work. Indeed, Nonentity can even serve to liberate cognition, to grant it possibilities that a mind repressing otherness can never experience: "If, for example, a man's ordinary mundane consciousness feels staggered at the improbability of an immaterial thinking-principle being the source of all things, Nonentity comes in and says, 'Contrasted with me, (that is, considered simply as *existent*) one principle is as probable as another' " (p. 61).

Belying its supposed nihilistic portents, Nonentity here performs the reverse of mental limitation: it lifts a commonsensical, object-oriented prohibition against believing in an immaterial First Cause and mocks the timid incredulity of a mundane mind. Setting a limit to what ordinary consciousness entertains as true, the specter of nonexistence undermines the absoluteness of any contention and opens a space for a revision of things. While each datum appears complete and whole, Nonentity sits beside it and marks its incompletion, its dynamic position in a wavering movement of being and nonbeing and otherness. Nonentity functions as an exteriority essential to any thing being brought into a field of experience. But Nonentity is itself never interiorized. A "parent of the philosophic craving" (*Essays in Philosophy,* 59), this basic involvement dislodges truth from the objects at hand and makes rationality a fluid propensity, not a binding agreement with those things. Nonentity shatters the simplicity of any given experience or reality, complicates the raw immediacy of present data. With this otherly mediation presiding over experience yet remaining inaccessible to cognition, the coerciveness of things and the plausibility of ideas become relative determinations, accessory facts no longer deciding mind's conclusions.

Belief, then, becomes a matter of probabilities, the latter determined pragmatically by the measure of fluidity that a principle provides. Without this otherness, cognition would pursue a single destiny or in fact would already be there. The universe would be totally immanent, the only things interfering with a total experience of the universe being empirical restrictions on how much can be thought at one time and in one place. Now everything can be experienced. It is just a matter of when and where mind gets around to doing so—or, rather, is *led* around to doing so, for, with no more beyond to point to, mind would always adhere to whatever object or idea is placed before it, would attach itself to the present and eliminate any further play of rationality. With metaphysical limits to thinking lifted, with no nonentity destabilizing mind's grounding in a putatively immediate experience, mind fluidly replicates the fluidity of phenomena, however dissatisfying that stream of objects might be. In such a world, mind would not function as mind, would no longer pursue a satisfying destiny, but instead would be carried along in a current of sensations. Mind would make no choices and draw no conclusions, for experience would involve a direct, obligatory correspondence of object and percept. To think, to carry out its essential function, mind must bear a degree of abstraction, a capacity to posit something besides what is given in sensation. But, to achieve abstraction, and the freedom that goes with it, mind needs some other thing or effect that limits the world at hand so that mind may withdraw from it. This is what otherness provides. Through otherness, mind assumes a reflective distance toward the things it encounters, now recognizing the world as such, as an as such and not as an absolute. If existence were all, if it had no other, then mind could not even think existence per se, could not even know it as a reality or concept. How could mind think existence, know what and how it is, unless mind knew what and how it is not, unless mind differentiated it, deprived it of universality?

Therefore, the assumption that a metaphysical limit to cognition inhibits cognition makes no sense, for this limit, this difference between knowable and unknowable, presence and absence, being and being's other (not just its opposite), is the place where thinking exercises. The fact that the "idea of Nonentity can . . . neither be exorcised nor identified" (*Essays in Philosophy,* 63) does not necessarily signify human inadequacy and cause ontological insecurity. Inadequacy and insecurity are, in fact, the result of attempting to exorcise otherness (the "boor's" method, James writes) or identify otherness (the *un*radical empiricist's method), of trying either to repress or to familiarize it. In ethical terms, mind feels impotent only when it fails to treat otherness as an instrument of freedom, when it interprets finitude as alienation, as the onset of annihilation. The idea of Nonentity helps thinkers incorporate otherness into any experience of brute facts, thereby gainsaying the usual materialistic, deterministic interpretations that hinder mind's quest for comfort. More specifically, contemplative minds abstain from factualizing otherness but still admit it as a constitutive element in human being, one that registers in consciousness not as a fact but as an emotion, a mysteriousness open to variations of mental adjustment.

To such minds, James continues in "The Sentiment of Rationality," "Existence will be a brute Fact to which as a whole the emotion of ontologic wonder shall rightfully cleave, but remain eternally unsatisfied. This wonderfulness or mysteriousness will then be an essential attribute of the nature of things, and the exhibition and emphasizing of it will always continue to be an ingredient in the philosophic industry of the race" (*Essays in Philosophy*, 63–64). Wonder and mystery, not truth or reality or revelation—that is the strange and inconclusive spark of thinking, the answer to and inspiration of the essay's opening question, "Why philosophize?" More than a subjective accompaniment to certain experiences, "ontologic wonder" reaches out to embrace the whole of existence, indeed, is the experience of existence as a whole, as a thing miraculously different from nonexistence. Hence, this emotion characterizes the most effective and comprehensive cognitive stances. While the idealist ignores brute fact and the traditional empiricist impoverishes the mysteriousness of things, the Jamesian mind marvels at the universe, sees objects clearly and feels them profoundly, sensing at the same time a metaphysical counterpart, an other unseen, a precognitive sentiment. The standard philosopher-scientist demands a sharp delineation of objects and their properties. His or her "theoretic rationality" covets simplicities, wants "the relief of identification" (p. 56), one *or* the other, entity *or* nonentity, not a tenuous apprehension of their concurrence and irresolution.

This interplay emerges as wonderfulness only after rationality is reconceived as a sentiment, after mind has ceased trying to appropriate or rationalize otherness and has instead begun to accept it. Forever concealed from systematizers and simplifiers, wonder is an affect of otherness withheld from substantiating gestures, of otherness maintained as other by a mind curious and open, grasping for bigger and better experiences yet fixating on no single object. And, even though wonder always touches on some thing beyond, the emotion still qualifies as empirical because it is not merely a derivative effect of experience, a secondary aesthetic response to a supposedly primary perception. Cleaving to all objects of thought, immanent everywhere, wonder is "an essential attribute of the nature of things"—*essence* here referring, not to *ousia,* but to whatever excites interest—and always part of an open mind's experience of things as such.[25]

So, contradicting the usual connotations of laxity, fuzziness, and obscurity, the presence of wonder signifies an active, thoughtful intelligence. If mind succumbs to epistemological conformity—"Most of us grow more and more enslaved to the stock conceptions with which we have once become familiar, and less and less capable of assimilating impressions in any but the old ways" (*Principles,* 754)—it can no longer feel wonder. Nor can it recognize a fresh experience, for an old way of assimilating renders all events familiar. But wonder engages a novel event *and* raises the possibility of a new mode of assimilation: "The relation of the new to the old, before the assimilation is performed, is wonder" (p. 754).

As preassimilative, wonder retains contact with that otherness inaccessible to old cognition. Hesitating at the threshold of assimilation, before mind's conceptual determinations are put to work, mind in wonder preserves old and new, familiar and unfamiliar, same and other, as a not quite fully cognized relation, a dynamic mediation not yet understood in such easy polarities as old and new. Wonder is the sensation of metaphysical difference, assimilation is the understanding of that difference, and the instance of wonder testifies to the inadequacy of that understanding. This is why wonder is not a form of satisfaction.

But, again, mind's cognitive shortcomings and its resort to wonder do not paralyze it, for inadequacy here is not a fallen, tragic, or nostalgic condition. A cognition may be adequate at least temporarily, if the concepts that mind has developed prove compatible with the experiences that it meets. But, while concepts do not change—"Conceptions form the one class of entities that cannot under any circumstances change" (*Principles,* 442)—experience does. So mind's clinging to the idea of a permanently satisfying concept is not tragic, merely perverse. This conceptual rigidity rules out wonder, indeed, casts wonder as a dangerous immersion in the metaphysical flux, as a mental stream emulating the natural continuum that concepts aim to control, to endow with sameness (see *Principles,* 434–42).

To satisfy at the same time the exigencies of changing sensation and the need for mental coherence, mind requires this wondering flexibility more than it does a set group of concepts. With the idea of Nonentity hovering over each existential position, all concepts are rendered context specific, provisional, no matter how much psychic investment they bear, and despite their initial absolutist claims ("Every thought is absolute to us at the moment of conceiving it or acting upon it" [*Essays in Philosophy,* 60]). No concept can exhaust the dynamic pull of otherness, so, as inertia invariably grows in conceptual thinking, the breach ever widens between mind's cognitive reserves and the experiences that outdistance them. Ontologic wonder cherishes this reduction, this relativizing of concepts, for it makes experience corrigible, exposes yesterday's conceptual inventions as today's dogma. More precisely, rather than being opposed to conceptuality per se, wonder happens at the point of otherness's historical appearance, between an experience already conceptualized and an experience not yet conceptualized, perhaps not assimilatable by the current inventory of concepts. It is a moment of compromise, an unfolding negotiation respecting conservative forces of mind yet admitting the progressive forces and disorienting effects of otherly encounters. As a relation, a mindfulness of nonentity that limits every previous datum, wonder anticipates a new organization of experience, a revision of things, even a self-revision. This latter possibility prevents one from interpreting wonder as a forestructuring of the world, whereby the network of relations constituting things is reoriented, leading to a new world and to new experiences. Such an interpretation shelters wonder from its own transformative results. But, because wonder is an event of differentiation, not an object or concept, because it is a moment of cognitive change, not a determined outcome, wonder can never solidify or recur.

Wonder itself changes, experiences the world differently each time. If it did not, it would become just as petrified and resistant as the concepts it mediates. If it were just a mental instrument, its mediating activity would settle into a repetitive pattern and mind would find itself trying to sustain obsolete habits in the face of new experiences it can interpret only as disruptive and uncanny. But wonder never occurs in quite the same way, for, even though mind can feel wonder over and over, wonder itself cannot be abstracted from the experiential flow, cannot be isolated or instrumentalized. Being a relation, not an identity, wonder is part of that flow, changing as the successive terms it relates changes. More important, wonder originates in and properly adheres to the beyond threshold, to the experience of the limit of being. Hence, any objectification of it implements the categories of being that wonder ungrounds. Since a particular experience can be wonderful once only—the second time already entails a loss of mysteriousness—its occasion manifests a mind's readiness to alter its thinking, to rechart its cognitive map. Neither shying away from nor trying to overcome otherness, wonder welcomes the latter's advent. In embracing otherness's defamiliarizing action, wonder happily converts uncanniness to exhilaration, disruption into re-creation. Mind then knows the (temporary) satisfaction of discovering new comprehensions, of bridging discordant states of mind, of lifting mind out of its commitment to a single concept, which is to say a single future (since concepts are teleological instruments).

This commanding and new relation is more than a simple juxtaposition of concepts. It has a transformative effect. While it is the case that "not new sensations . . . but new conceptions, are the indispensable conditions of advance," the recognition and use of a conception as new rests on its coming about in a new relation: "The new truth affirms in every case a *relation* between the original subject of conception and some new subject conceived later on" (*Principles*, 439). This between must possess a dynamic, synthetic force, for concepts in themselves, maintained as discrete, yield nothing but a reapplication and the same assimilation. A mere recombination of concepts yields, not a new truth, but only a different order or arrangement of the old and insufficient truths. Simply adding some new subject to the existing subjects may add content to mind's fund of knowledge, but it does not reshape those contents into a more satisfying interpretation of things, nor does it inspire any wondrous apprehension. Thinking "this plus this" or thinking "this then this" affirms nothing except the two conceived subjects and their contiguity, and contiguity does not demand any new conceptualization or relativizing of the subjects. However, "if two of them are thought at once, their *relation* may come to consciousness, and form matter for a third conception" (p. 440).

Relation, therefore, is the place of progress, wonder the sign of its novelty, otherness the perpetuity of movement. What is unrelated is grounded, immobile, absolute: "The Absolute is what has not yet been transcended, criticized or made relative" (*Essays in Philosophy*, 60). A mind pursuing absolutes flees relation and otherness and, therefore, advancement. Because it is always possible that "the notion of nonentity may blow in from the infinite and extinguish the theoretic rationality of a universal datum" (p. 60), an absolutist mind can guard itself against relativism only by embracing ever narrower conceptions and broader exclusions. But a mind seeking otherness yet suspecting universal conclusions passes through ever more liberal conceptions of being. With each wonderful experience, mind encounters a different metaphysic. Welcoming otherness as an inspiration for growth, not as a threat to stability, mind relinquishes the quest for absolute knowledge, thereby avoiding what James considers Hegel's great mistake: trying to eliminate all "conceivable outlying notions" so that "the whole of possible thought" may circulate within the "bounds" of an "adamantine unity" (p. 59). To James, this "logical bridge" that Hegel draws between "Nonentity and Being" functions as a repression, not as a realization, a futile effort since any attempt to assimilate Nonentity to Being solicits the categories of Being to which Nonentity is exterior.

Of course, there are provisional others to familiarize or negate or become familiarized to—those processes make up life. To these transformations James addresses the majority of his writings, often assuming the posture of scientist or psychologist, arguing as if he has forgotten his metaphysical insight. However, that does not mean that James believes that he can ever settle the meaning of otherness. Even when his language affirms identities uncritically, James often inserts cautionary statements reiterating the conventionality of those identities.[26] He remains mindful of the fact that incorporating all "outlying notions" into habitual thinking, familiarizing otherness absolutely and believing in the viability and justness of that end, is to submit all other existences and lives to a single conception. This arrogance often passes for vision, for a universal understanding of things rightly transcending the limits of local knowledge. It wants to be unrelative, unrelated, but in so doing it precludes its own advancement. It consigns itself to isolation, minimizes its experiential possibilities. In constituting all others as finite, a Hegelian mind projects all its experiences as finite, fully containable by predetermined assimilations.

But, paradoxically, a mind knowing its own locality enjoys an expanding receptivity. Like a Hegelian mind, a Jamesian mind never actually obtains a unified prospect, a totally appropriated world. However, by forsaking the former's dream of complete immanence, by recognizing the infinite backdrop of alterity against which any locality emerges, a Jamesian mind anticipates vaster, happier, farther, and closer beyonds than does a mind hoping to consume the backdrop itself. Thought becomes a series of tenuous negotiations and amendments, a "constant play of furtherances and hindrances" (*Principles,* 286). Apprehending infinite otherness, mind becomes infinitely restless, captivated by that " 'fringe' of unarticulated affinities" (p. 250) trailing every present thing, transforming all local others into material to grow through, not recoil from or subdue.

Herein lies William James's pragmatic constitution of thinking, his metaphysical solution to the severe cognitive demands placed on an acquisitive, desirous, inquiring modern consciousness.[27] Whether William's meandering, detailed psychological and philosophical speculations actually or directly arise from or respond to the American situation as described by Henry is a precarious historical question. In any case, it is clear that Henry's program for a new synthetic, creative achievement requires an innovation in consciousness, a mental adjustment that his characters often fail to achieve but that William's elucidations of this new thinking prophesy. He avoids the novelist's American characters' epistemological mistakes by broaching otherness as a necessary, appropriate, yet unobjectifiable condition of momentous thinking. This progressive synthetic thinking thrives by being drawn to whatever reduces its thoughts to relativity. Any new experience, any wonder-producing otherness that finitizes a concept previously held to be universal captivates Henry's American and William's pragmatic mind and, strangely enough, amplifies it. Although mind never wholly masters otherness, the latter's incessant beyond effect still serves mind as an emancipating mechanism, sheltering mind from the fatal attraction that Henry's characters often suffer: outgrowing the provinciality of the American scene only to be submerged in just another locality. The properly oriented pragmatic mind surpasses any conditional assimilation of otherness, any occasional appropriation of the new, for this happy achievement is temporalized as soon as otherness exercises its destabilizing pull. Mind finds itself rationalizing each new disturbance, feeling out new parameters of experience, in which old ones are retained as relative parts. This progress never ends, but it is the only attitude or orientation in which the Jamesian, pragmatic, prospective mind finds its fulfillment.

Notwithstanding James's empiricist reputation, and contrary to recent characterizations by neopragmatists of James's pragmatism in political and institutional terms, his pragmatism begins with a metaphysical experience, a psychic apprehension. Wonder, Otherness, Nonentity, the Sentiment of Rationality—these are the elements driving the revisionary pragmatic method that James outlines in his later works. Not the only elements, surely, but crucial ones, such liminal phenomena lie at the heart of James's principles of psychology and legitimate his psychologically grounded pragmatism. Although wonder et al. do not appear directly in James's official pragmatic essays, their cognitive effects as outlined in "The Sentiment of Rationality" and *The Principles of Psychology* sanction the overriding goal of the later pragmatic writings, namely, an adjustment of existing realities. Specifically, Jamesian pragmatism's scheme of concrete alterations in beliefs and behaviors presupposes mind's wondering experience of nonentity, its willingness to entertain otherness. Pragmatic change starts with a cognitive attitude toward novelty, alterity, the beyond. This attitude does not resist otherly manifestations, nor does it prize them for themselves. Rather, it takes them as an enabling condition of mind's capaciousness, an instrument for cognitive growth.

On this experiential approach to things depend the political consequences hailed by contemporary critics.[28] The pluralism that James advocates as both a scientific method and an ethical stance (and that neopragmatists single out as a political good) requires an otherness effect in order to relativize any monism. The recognition of choice in the worlds that we create follows from the wonder that we feel at certain ontological moments. The spurious objectivity of certain forms of rationalism (plus, according to the neopragmatist, the dubious politics that go along with them) becomes clear once we recast rationality itself as a sentiment. This is to say that, while neopragmatist interpretations like those discussed in the preface spotlight the political implications of standard pragmatic sayings (e.g., "meaning equals consequences," "theory is but one form of practice") and often attribute them to James, in fact, in James's writings, those principles rest on a condition of mind. Mind's ability to experience the world along the lines of wonder and otherness are necessary to the routine adjustments that mind makes in its cognitive course. For this reason, a political interpretation of James's pragmatism, one expelling the metaphysical side of cognition from pragmatic conduct, is incomplete. A pragmatic outlook of pluralism and anticorrespondence requires a pragmatic state of mind embracing provisional belief and revisionary habits. Such provisions and revisions are forced on an open mind as soon as wonder arrives to shake mind's inertia, as soon as nonentity comes to deuniversalize present existents, as soon as a sentiment of fluidity overpowers our search for truth. For James, this psychometaphysical condition is pragmatism's source and ally. Pragmatic method is its best expression.

Chapter Three

Peirce's Logic of Pragmatic Inference

If we follow James's precepts regarding philosophical inquiry, we cannot take his adjustment of cognition as a final conclusion. Even if James's pragmatic psychology advocates an experiential openness, a posture of thoughtful inconclusiveness, it still posits a *conclusion* of inconclusiveness. That is, this processual psychic condition is not to be identified with a meandering stream of consciousness, a pure, free-floating ego randomly passing through experience, abandoning itself to flux. Selection, attention, habit formation continue, always with concrete ends in mind. Otherness does not curtail anticipations of satisfaction. It does not render absurd any directions given to the stream. Rather, otherness (once reinterpreted) prevents those anticipations from settling into a static, narrow mode of thinking, into a desire for repetition that ultimately can maintain life only as a series of unpleasant surprises. So mind does not avoid fruitless and dissatisfying repetition by positing a pure inconclusiveness. Instead, mind remains productive by testing one conclusion against another, by bringing to light the consequences of any belief, the practical outcome that contextualizes and limits any putative absolute, even the absolute that there are no absolutes. It does so by

never fearing to ask the pragmatic question: in this case, What specific effects does James's concept of mental progress yield? What satisfactions, what beliefs, what habits, result when otherness provisionalizes
experience?

The purpose of Jamesian thinking is to enable an individual mind to
enjoy an expanding comprehensiveness. The rationale is simple: the wider
mind's cognitions are, the less it will be upset by life's transitions. A mind
disinclined to relinquish prior conceptions can only halt in the face of a
new fact or an odd experience. Instead of reorienting itself, such a mind
represses the strangeness of the object or fact and shrinks back into yesterday's understanding, a strategy that James claims cannot, in the long run,
be sustained. But a Jamesian mind recognizes that the genuinely new
marks a limit to the (now) old way of thinking, that being dislodged from
one mental resting place, although painful, merely prepares mind to meet
that strange experience the next time without shock. Otherness (and the
pain it causes) actually ameliorates the future by coercing mind into discovering ever more capacious thoughts. Although these thoughts do not
shelter one from emotional pain, they do bring that pain to an understanding and prevent it from causing intellectual pain, cognitive confusion. In
answer to the questions posed above, then, satisfaction depends on the
roominess of mind's concepts, mind's readiness to broach difference and
divest itself of unworkable beliefs, mind's habituating itself to change. This
is how thought progresses.

But, again, despite mind's liberality, thought's progress is not without
direction or determination. In fact, as James defines cognition in *The
Principles of Psychology,* not only thought's momentary groundings but also
its general progress remain forever contained by an absolute structure.
Notwithstanding James's emphasis on mental motion and conceptual
openness, one formal element in his cognitive model does not change.
Because *"Thought tends to Personal Form"* (*Principles,* 220), cognitive ad-
vances always take place within the frame of a single and personal mind.
The personal form may expand, but it can never grow beyond itself, for
"every 'thought' is part of a personal consciousness" (p. 220), and "no thought
even comes into direct *sight* of a thought in another personal consciousness
than its own. Absolute insulation, irreducible pluralism, is the law. . . .
The breaches between such thoughts are the most absolute breaches in
nature" (p. 221). There is no such thing as *a* thought—it is always *my*

thought or *your* thought or *her* thought. And, because *"Thought is in Constant Change"* (p. 224), not to mention the fact that selfhood is partly physiologically based (see *Principles,* 286–88), these different loci of thinking can never produce identical cognitions, nor can they share a cognitive experience. They may think the same object, but differences in human bodies, sensations, memories, perspectives, and so on render the experience of that object different from person to person and, within one personal mind, from moment to moment. Were I to try to cognize your cognition, I would fail, for the intentional structure of cognition means that I can know your cognition only as an *object* of my cognition.[1] And to know subjects only as objects of thought is, first, to make a subject's acts of cognition into objects and, then, to convert those objects into objects of thought—a double breach that no psychological strategy can correct. This ultimate breach may help structure thought's development, but in so doing it only maintains the essential immobility of the intersubjective relation. With all cognitions secured in a personal closed-mindedness, absolute insulation is the law, the condition that obscures every other consciousness.

The question is, Can the utter sightlessness of an other thought serve as an effective instrument or inspiration of my thought's growth? If remote stars are less otherly than other minds, if rocks and stones and trees are more available to consciousness than other consciousnesses are, then thinking's best occasion for expansion should be the latter, for the more unfamiliar the otherness facing mind is, the more expansion and adaptability mind can achieve in surpassing it. But, because thought's growth can take place only in and as a mind's extension, to surpass this limit, to know other minds and recognize their cognitions, would entail, not mind's greater expansions, but mind's disintegration. As the inescapable province of cognition, personal consciousness stands as a structural necessity preventing mind from thinking outside its personal enclosure. This is one limit that does not lead mind beyond its present capacity. On the contrary, it only throws every cognition striving to assimilate this particular other back on itself.

At this point, mind's progress stops. Although progress continues in other regions, when faced with demands, requests, disturbances, and so on originating in another consciousness, mind reaches an existential quandary. By definition, its ability to handle those coercions, to incorporate them into its inclusive cognition, is what maintains consciousness as an identity, a discrete bundle of experiences. Yet the discreteness and enclosure of the one consciousness implies the discreteness and enclosure of the other—paradoxically, these consciousnesses' mutual reflection keeps them apart, supports them in a reciprocal isolation. Even if this separation-limitation were a matter of choice and not one of necessity, the same outcome would hold, for, if one consciousness were somehow able to incorporate the other, then the other would be able to incorporate the one. Therefore, to pursue and assimilate an other mind, to break down its structural integrity, would be to imperil one's own integrity, to portend one's mental destruction. Here, consciousness arrives at a self-contradiction, an internal resistance to progress: to preserve itself as a process of expanding cognitions, consciousness must not coalesce with another consciousness. That is to say, cognition so defined cannot and must not search for a new way of knowing that other, of making it its own. Not only would that incorporation destroy that triangulation of mind–object–other mind that grounds our suppositions about objectivity (*Principles,* 262), but it would destroy the minds as well. When my consciousness encounters an otherness in the form of a parallel consciousness, a set of rival "elementary psychic fact[s]" (p. 221) reflecting yet "othering" mine, my consciousness must suspend the activity keeping it vital.

This attitude is the opposite of the cognitive openness that James counsels, the willingness to abandon (if necessary) any and all intellectual commitments in the presence of a novel fact or inconsistent conclusion. Shying away from this cognitive threshold, mind constitutes any further cognitive enlargement as an addition of content, a gathering of information under the purview of a personal subject structure, not the advent of a new impersonal knowledge or a new intersubjectivity. Confronted with an otherness that it can assimilate only by risking its own existence, by puncturing its own grounding insulation, James's personal consciousness sticks to self-confirming habits of thought, limiting itself to minding experiential data that it can admit without danger. This amounts to a repression—not a redirection of the stream, or a conceptual adjustment, but a simple collapse of mind's method, a stoppage. An other mind functions, not as a springboard but as a dead end, a pseudo-object that will not be conceptualized into a teleological instrument. And, because consciousness subsists in flux, any absolute bar to cognition cannot remain benign. It enters consciousness as a dynamic interruption, a vacant space of antiexperience pressing for accommodation.

This dead-endedness must not be interpreted as a property of an other mind, particularly as one signifying the ultimate ineptitude of consciousness. Rather, it is one logical outcome of James's operative postulates and assumptions about cognition. Given mind's personal *savoir,* all minds remain eternally segregated, mutually unknowable—there is no changing that. But, although the breach between them is unbridgeable, it is still a relation, a relation in which mind is intimately involved and one that belies the supposed extraneousness of the other term in the relation. Holding cognitions together in and as disparateness, this breach relation contradicts the absolute disconnection of consciousnesses. Or, rather, it modifies the meaning of insulation, for the fact that one consciousness cannot know another, that one can cognize the other's cognition only as a *cogitandum,* is not a derivative consequence or side effect of the principles of psychology. This exclusionary relation is essential to consciousness, not a circumstance on which consciousness stumbles. Being unable to know what goes on inside another mind and to fuse with it is precisely what grants a mind its integrity and singularity. "Absolute insulation" forces the recognition that consciousness can be conscious only within a structure of intersubjective breaches, a field of shadowy counterparts that it senses but that it can process simply as objects, not as other processing consciousnesses. That "there is no giving or bartering between [thoughts]" (*Principles,* 221) does not mean that consciousness is complete and sufficient unto itself. This withholding is a defining attribute of the world in which consciousness exists.

That is to say, what James casts as irreducible pluralism is, at the same time, a basic factor in consciousness's singularity. What appears to be an outer, otherly existence is also an inner necessity, a constitutive exteriority marking the limit enabling mind to carry out its acts. Without other minds' absolute exteriority, no mind could exist or constitute itself as an absolute interiority, as a subjective intelligence interiorizing objects. In other words, other minds' irreducible otherness is essential to any particular mind's identity, wholeness, and personality. So, given that the personal form of one consciousness rests on a personalizing differentiation of one consciousness from another, that an other personal form is the precondition for the one, that mind's personality does not originate wholly from within, we must hold off taking personality as a psychological given or starting point. Unless mind admits the other's functional inaccessibility, mind destines itself to trying to uphold a spurious independence. In making futile, blind efforts to overcome one condition of its efforts, mind mistakenly fetishizes its intersubjective relations, regards them as static encounters, not as constitutive positionings. To accord with James's injunction that every relation be relative, not absolute, James's own definition of thought as transpiring in a discrete personal form must be criticized (but not dismissed). His notion of "every thought being *owned*" (*Principles*, 221), being proper to a personal consciousness, must give way to a revised understanding of the construction of thought, one that makes the incommunicability of any *cogitatio* an essential constituent of personal consciousness.

The only way this revised understanding of mind can work through James's dilemma of (in a word) psychologism, the only way it can turn the intersubjective standstill into an occasion for growth, is to incorporate this subjective otherness into the structure of each respective thought. It must develop a slightly different theory of cognition, one that converts James's confrontational situation between consciousnesses, whereby my fully formed thought relates to others' fully formed thoughts through inevitable misidentifications, into a dialectical situation within consciousness, whereby the formation of my thoughts rests on a reference to some other to which they can never become identical. The former theory pictures one regnant personal consciousness personalizing the world around it and subsuming other personalities merely as objects, not as persons. But, by recalling that mind requires other persons for it to become personal, the latter theory translates this interpersonal rivalry into an intrapersonal relation, a cognitive structure. This kind of cognition contains an other cognition not personally contained. The latter is not opposed to the former, or barred from it, but rather part of the former's constitution. Or, rather than speaking of *containment* or *partness,* terms that suggest that the latter can be reduced to the former, we must consider a thought as an address, a pointing beyond itself, a cognitive being becoming itself through and as this pointing to some other. And that other is not another personal consciousness, but another thought understood in the same referential manner. In this line of reasoning, cognition is no longer a connection of dissimilar monads—personal thought cognizing impersonal objects. It is a general forward-looking process of indication, a distribution of thought gestures. And in that dynamic structure we do not have some preexistent thought referring to some preexistent other—rather, thinking and personality arise in and as this act of reference.

Clearly, this is to redefine thought and cognition, to interpret those terms no longer psychologically, but now semiotically, for the only thing that is by referring to something else is the sign. And, if we wish to pursue a theory of cognition as semiosis, we must bracket James's psychological premises and take up the pragmaticist conjectures of his friend, mentor, dependent, muse, gadfly: Charles Sanders Peirce. It is Peirce who quickly recognizes that James's definition of psychology as "the science of finite individual minds" (*Principles,* 6) presupposes a fundamental object of study: personal consciousness, a substantialized dynamic psyche that undergoes various physical, emotional, and perceptual changes. In a word, Peirce criticizes James for positing a personal basis for the nature of cognition. James forthrightly claims to develop a psychology of mental states that takes the personal self as "the immediate datum in psychology" (p. 221), but, in a discussion of James's *Principles of Psychology,* Peirce qualifies that personal self as an "illusory phenomenon," as a "delusion" of "isolated existence."[2] Peirce claims that he is "particular to avoid" such "psychological distinctions" (*Semiotic and Significs,* 31), since they uncritically take a personal psyche as the ground of those distinctions, not something to be analyzed and distinguished. To Peirce, what makes the personal self a faulty supposition is not only an ethical imperative to ask the "question whether there is anything of any more dignity, worth, and importance than individual happiness, individual aspirations, and individual life" (*W,* 2:487).[3] Nor is his assertion of the illusoriness of personal selfhood based on some transindividual psychological instinct, some "social impulse" (see *W,* 3:250) that draws minds to others and may even be constitutive of mind.[4] Fundamentally, what leads James into overemphasizing the personal dimension of consciousness, what forces Peirce to counter James's psychologizing with assertions about the public nature of truth, the communal method of inquiry, and the consensual status of reality, is James's insistence on interpreting cognition itself within the boundaries of a finite individual mind.

If the personal self is to serve as an immediate datum for psychology, its most fundamental experiences must be entirely self-contained, structured by the mental boundaries of personal consciousness. The personal self's root cognitions should take the form of an unmediated relation of mind and object. If an other mind or a transindividual concept or any impersonal factor participates from the start in any mind's particular cognition, then personal consciousness can neither serve psychology as its basic object of study nor stand as the ground of human being. An external relation would seem to participate from the start in any cognitive process and so would have to be accounted for in the development of any putatively enclosed identity. But, for James, this is not the case, for, even when mind thinks several things and thoughts together, even when it faces a "blooming, buzzing confusion" of sensations, it does so "*in a single pulse of subjectivity, a single psychosis, feeling, or state of mind,*" for "*however complex the object may be, the thought of it is one undivided state of consciousness*" (*Principles,* 268, 266). (Here James is trying to counter associationist psychology and its notion of cognition as a "fusion of appearances" that are "really separate.")

In an 1866 manuscript "On a Method of Searching for the Categories," Peirce names this single, irreducible mental act an *impression.* A synonym for *intuition, impression* signifies an "*immediate cognition,*" "an ultimate fact" underived from any previous knowledge. It is "a premiss not itself a conclusion, an empirical constituent of knowledge not itself containing nonempirical parts" (*W,* 1:515). As a knowledge relation composed solely of physical object and mental representation, an impression involves no act of comparison or discrimination, for, if it did, then it would presuppose an externality necessary to the internalization of sensuous contents. But, according to James's cognitive assumptions, any discrimination that mind makes is due to mind's own filtering mechanism, the selectiveness determined by mind's physique (brain, nerves, and so on) and the object's coerciveness, not by an appeal to conceptions or categories. At this brute level of experience, mind merely registers the raw data that come before it. True, as James affirms, mind thinks that sensuous tumult wholly, an integration that might seem to indicate a referring of sensations to organizing categories not inherent in the datum itself. But, actually, a Jamesian mind's unifying activity rests not on the implementation of a category that orients sensation into an intelligible whole, but on mind's own capacity to function as that orientation, as a point of reference for the chaos around it. Mind experiences impressions as impressions, not by referring them to something outside the direct mind-object relation, but by being a co-herent, unique entity to which things are referred.

The presence of impressions as such, therefore, presupposes a working individual mind, an undivided personal self. A concrete, especial cognition, an impression contains nothing not immediately present to mind and operative in mind. The singularity of a particular impression signifies the singularity of the mind experiencing it and the personal basis of that experience. At the level of impressions, an "empirical correlation" obtains between mental and physical or, as James puts it, between "various sorts of thought or feeling [and] definite conditions of the brain" (*Principles,* 6). And restraining itself to describing that empirical happening is what makes psychology scientific, for "all attempts to *explain* our phenomenally given thoughts as products of some deeper-lying entities . . . are metaphysical" (p. 6).

But what is a "phenomenally given thought"? An "impression"? Very well, but how do we know that it is an impression? Are experiencing an impression and knowing that it is an impression that we are experiencing one and the same mental act? Is the latter also an impression, an impression tacked on to the first impression, yet just as given? If an impression assumes the status of a first knowledge, a knowledge unconditioned by any other knowledge, only after a second knowledge comes along to predicate the first knowledge with firstness, then what becomes of the impression's wholeness, its ultimate character? Is wholeness of thought mind's first condition, or is wholeness itself determined by other processes, by relations more fundamental than Jamesian cognition's personal nature?

These are the initial questions that Peirce raises in his early interrogations (during the years 1866–69) of an impression- or intuition-based model of cognition and a personal self-based psychology of thinking. Peirce asks these questions in the light of a particular premise: that having an impression and knowing that what we are having is an impression are two distinct mental events. With this distinction clarified—that "it is plainly one thing to have an intuition and another to know intuitively that it is an intuition" (*W,* 2:194)—the question becomes whether we can intuitively distinguish an impression, recognize it without the introduction of a nonintuitive element. Can mind know an impression impressionably, using only the materials of the present thing? In the "Categories" manuscript, Peirce answers, "No one can know what an impression is like, in itself: for a recognized difference between two impressions would be a difference between them *as compared,* that is, as mediately known, and not between them *in themselves.* An impression in itself is an uncomprehended impression, and hence, an undifferentiated sensation, like the feeling of our heart's motion" (*W,* 1:515).

"No one can *know* what an impression is like, in itself," because an impression by definition precedes the activation of a framework of knowledge (save the structure of vision, hearing, and so on) and knowing exceeds the impression known. Knowing it means knowing it *as,* recognizing this content as an instance of a general condition—pure immediacy, immediacy being a category of existence not itself given immediately. Knowing what an impression is like implies a comparison, an attribution of resemblance to and difference from other experiences falling in the same category of immediate isness. And that comparison involves more than just setting two things side by side, for the things come to be recognized as comparable data only in and through that comparison, that principle or act of differentiation that signifies a third, non-thing-like element necessary to the comparison of the two things. Without some basis of comparison, some unifying standard or concept—"two ideas are compared only in the idea of a class, lot, or set to which they belong" (*CP,* 7.392)—impressions remain incomprehensible, vague, unrelated. Each new impression needs to be placed into likeness with other experiential contents, else it remains wholly unique, unlimited, incomparable, an event ultimate and indeterminate (in that it relates to nothing).

This does not mean that impressions do not happen. It means that, in order to talk about them, think about them, recognize them while we are having them, indeed, to decide whether they do or do not exist, we must distinguish them, predicate them with the quality of impressionness, and that predication is not itself an impression. Because "predicates are mediate cognitions" (*W,* 1:517), they cannot be impressions, for every predication works by propositions, that is, by the connection of a subject with a predicate, a connection presuming a knowledge of that predicate, an awareness external to the data present. Thus, our knowledge of the impression (the subject) being an impression (the predicate) is mediated by an understanding of not this or that impression but impression in general. And "impression in general or as such, is itself by virtue of its generality not an impression but a conception" (p. 516). For a mind to know impressions, then,

> they need to be reduced by the understanding to the unity of consistency and therefore to be combined, and that not by chaotic aggregation but in a determinate form. This form or way of combining impressions is an element of cognition not given in the impressions combined, but added to them in order to reduce them to the requisite unity. It is, therefore, a *hypothetically* adjoined element; for a hypothesis is something assumed in order to reduce an otherwise incomprehensible *datum* to unity. This element of cognition is termed *conception*. (p. 516)

A hypothesis is an assumption, one that renders experience coherent, that makes sensations experienceable. Tentative and provisional, hypotheses play an explanatory role in experience, one evaluated here by what beneficial cognitive effects can be gained from them.[5] In behavioristic terms, which Peirce elsewhere opts for, the best cognitive outcome would be an explanation that can "supply a proposition which, if it had been known to be true before the phenomenon presented itself, would have rendered that phenomenon predictable" (*CP,* 7.191). In epistemological terms, a good hypothesis "renders that phenomenon rational" (par. 191). Indeed, this interpretation of hypotheses as ways of combining impressions into intelligible wholes is itself hypothetical: Peirce assumes the existence and effect of a hypothesis precisely because it is the only way he can rationally account for that coherence. Impressions by themselves do not cohere—they appear only in "chaotic aggregation." And a mere piling together of impressions does not constitute a unity. Mind requires a "determinate form" if it is going to embrace impressions into a "unity of consistency," and even in that formative act a hypothesis has already been made, namely, that "these are impressions."

Hypotheses serve one purpose: to transform incomprehension into comprehension. Again, dropping the Kantian language of "understanding," "categories," and "manifold" and adopting the behavioristic language of Peirce's later "The Fixation of Belief," we can say that hypotheses convert that "uneasy and dissatisfied state" called "doubt" into that "calm and satisfactory state" called "belief" (*W,* 3:247). Sometimes—when he says, for example, that "an explanation is needed when facts contrary to what we should expect emerge" (*CP,* 7.202)—Peirce implies that doubt and a concomitant hypothesis occur after the fact. But the most rudimentary doubt is this pre- or nonfactual condition. Hypothesis begins at a level of basic incomprehension—not the uncertainty of, say, whether something exists, whether a proposition is true or false, or whether an act is moral or immoral, but the breakdown of cognition, mind's failure to understand what some thing is, although it may be present to sense. Of course, thingness and presentness are themselves determinations and mark an at least partially successful cognition. Likewise, as the other of comprehension, incomprehension is itself a determination.

The problem is that *incomprehensible* is a predicate that does not lead to any further cognitions, that does not admit any more clarifying or unifying hypotheses. An "incomprehensible *datum*" is an incomplete, dead-end cognition, an interruption in the procession of experiences. It cannot be derived from, carried over to, or compared or contrasted with any other experiences, for mind possesses no other category to apply to it and make it consistent and recognizable. An incomprehensible experience has no relation to anything else, or, rather, its only relation is difference, incongruity, disrelation. And, because "whatever we know, we know only by its relations, and insofar as we know its relations" (*W*, 2:164), our entire thought of and discourse about an incomprehensible experience falls into a blank, uninformative, dissatisfying repetition of its incomprehensibility. Mind cannot even understand what it is about that phenomenon that makes it incomprehensible, only that the predicate implies a subject, a comprehension of the subject as capable of receiving the term *incomprehensible.*

In a sense, then, there is no pure but only partial incomprehensibility. What is often assumed to be the fundamental incomprehensibility—the chaotic, random flux of sensation—is actually an initial comprehension, a first organization of experience. Mind cannot really experience randomness, irregularity, discontinuity, all such modes of incomprehension: "Irregularity . . . cannot be expected, as such. For an expectation is, in every case, founded upon some regularity" (*CP*, 7.191). Such qualifications of sense experience merely give a consistently random, regularly irregular character to sense impressions. As opposed to some raw, unformed material that mind cognizes, sense impressions are a function of cognition, a horizon marking "the limit of cognition" (*W*, 2:191), suggesting what there was before mind began its conceptual work. But this preconceptual moment is a functional hypothesis, not a reality, the postulation of immediate contact with things that coincides with the cognition of things' relations, significance, causes, and consequences. Sense impressions stand on the other side of intelligibility. They are necessary to intelligible content's advent, for intelligible content implies unintelligible or preintelligible impressions, that which mind renders intelligible. Even predicating an object with the character of intelligibility means conceiving of an unintelligible object. Even though, by definition, an unintelligible object does not exist, the concept of it is requisite to the concept of intelligible object: "All determination is by negation; we can first recognize any character whatsoever only by putting an object which first possesses it into comparison with an object which possesses it not. A conception, therefore, which was quite universal in every respect would be unrecognizable and impossible" (*W,* 2:231).

The thing that mind must remember is that it grasps the existence of sense impressions not through another impression but through an inference, one resting on an understanding of the concept *impression,* for "any reflection upon an impression, since it is a step towards bringing it to the unity of consistency, is a conception" (*W,* 1:517). In conceiving impressions, cognition goes beyond the given data. Indeed, cognition is precisely this going beyond the present fact, present facts having the character of presence and facticity only after mind has conceptualized them. Again, that does not mean that present facts do not exist, only that mind comprehends them through a mediate cognition, a cognition that supervenes the immediate data that it purports to cognize. This mental method forces the suspension of the question of whether impressions and things are real. Their ontological status gives way to their cognitive character. In the light of Peirce's distinction between having an impression and knowing it, the pertinent questions are, How does this conceptualization of nonconceptual things come about? Given that the content of each particular impression is unique, how do impressions become consistent and recognizable? In other words, inquiry into mind's workings properly asks, not about an impression's reality, but about an impression's cognizability.[6]

An impression becomes cognizable once it matches up with a conception, a classification that renders the impression consistent with and comparable to other impressions. (Of course, the first classification here is *impression.*) Even a singular phenomenon, an experience ostensibly unique and unfamiliar, accords with a general category of singularity within which the phenomenon's singularity may be differentiated from the singularity of other singular phenomena. True, "those things which we call singulars exist, but the character of singularity which we attribute to them is self-contradictory" (*W,* 2:181); "the true individual term, the absolutely singular *this* and *that* cannot be reached. Whatever has comprehension must be general" (*W,* 1:461).

However, this matching of impression and conception, the attribution of a "character" to a "singular"—none of these connections can happen as only a two-part relation, for nothing in the terms taken by themselves can facilitate and guarantee their correspondence. By definition, impressions do not relate to anything, and conceptions, being "hypotheses" that "go beyond the immediate fact itself" (*W,* 1:517) but that do not contain any inherent rule of correctness or appropriateness to that fact, can always be misapplied. Neither the impression nor the conception bears the criterion of its correspondence to the other within itself. Impressions do not automatically point toward a particular conception, nor does a conception automatically subsume pertinent impressions. Therefore, their unification requires a third term, or, rather, not merely a term but a function or an act, one that constitutes these elements of cognition both as terms related to each other. Mind may perhaps conceive conceptions and be impressed by impressions, but both mental acts are only partial and hypothetical cognitions, since an entirely unimpressionable conception and an entirely unconceptualized impression are experiential impossibilities. To cognize anything is to bring a concept and an impression together. However, to conceive a particular impression, or to know an impression as exemplifying a certain conception, mind must posit that connection, however unconsciously or instantaneously. And, since every cognitive gesture involves comparison, discrimination, and so on, since every "this represents this" implies "this does not represent that," mind links impression to conception by recalling something external but somehow related to the two given terms. And the externality's relation of relevance holds only insofar as the impression and conception are related (or relatable). Impression and conception become cognizable in and through this reference, and the third term can become referable only if the first two are connectable. This is why it makes no sense to talk about any of these terms as existing independently. Cognition involves a judgment—"this represents this"—but, "because the subject of any judgment must have been known by *collateral* acquaintance" (*Semiotic and Significs,* 72), that is, by a previous acquaintance with a similar *that* rendering *this* recognizable, each term is irreducibly relative. Every coupling of impression-conception, particular-general, and so on partakes in a triangular relation, and each term becomes itself by relating to the other term, and it relates to the other only if another term represents them as related: "A thing cannot stand for something without standing *to* something *for* that something" (*W,* 1:466). This organizing cognitive moment turns on a reference "*to,*" an appeal beyond the impression-conception dualism, the recipient of this reference being one of Peirce's most ingenious conceptions, the "interpretant"—"Reference to an interpretant, is simply the *addressing* of an impression to a conception" (*W,* 1:523; an entire section of the 1866 "Searching for the Categories" manuscript is devoted to the interpretant).[7]

"Addressing" is a connection brought about by something other than the terms connected. However, this does not suggest that the interpretant and the terms addressed preexist the reference. The interpretant does not so much show the consistency, comparability, or compatibility of diverse parts and moments of experience as it renders those parts and moments consistent, comparable, compatible—in a word, experienceable. That is, until referred to an interpretant, things presented to mind remain unrecognized, not yet understood, and cognition proper does not even begin:

> Suppose, we look out the word *homme* in a French dictionary; we shall find opposite to it the word *man,* which, so placed, represents *homme* as representing the same two-legged creature which *man* itself represents. In a similar way, it will be found that every comparison requires, besides the related thing, the ground and the correlate, also a *mediating representation which represents the relate to be a representation of the same correlate which this mediating representation itself represents.* Such a mediating representation, I call an *interpretant,* because it fulfills the office of an interpreter who says that a foreigner says the same thing which he himself says. (*W,* 1:523)

Peirce's technical description of "relate," "correlate," and "interpretant" interacting through relations of "representation" and "comparison" invites the supposition that the three terms exist independently of those relations. But there is no "correlate" (here, the concept *two-legged creature*) without a "relate" (the word *homme*), and there is no correspondence

between them without an "interpretant" (*man*) to establish and corrobo-
rate that correspondence. Peirce's terms function as positions, not sub-
stances, or, rather, their substantiation rests on the mediation of the others.
This is why, in his italicized summation, Peirce repeats the word *represents*
five times. Each term comes into existence, emerges as an object of cognition, only as it represents and is represented by the other two. Earlier and
later, Peirce defines *interpretant* as the same circular operation—"by an
interpretant we mean a representation which represents that something is a
representation of something else of which it is itself a representation" (*W*,
1:474); "the object of representation can be nothing but a representation of
which the first representation is the interpretant" (*CP*, 1.339)—a seemingly redundant activity that is nevertheless necessary to cognitive processing. Until *man* represents *homme* as a representation of what *man* itself
represents—*two-legged creature*—the word *homme* remains uncognized, the
concept *two-legged creature* unrepresented, the word *man* unutilized.

Why is this so? Why can cognition not take place without an appeal to
an "interpreter," a mediating representation external to the impression-
conception pairing? Once again, because an impression is not cognizable
until it has been rendered consistent with other impressions, that consistency resting on the impression's being addressed to a conception that links
it to (now) similar impressions. Alone and unrelated, not cohering with
anything else, appearing seemingly out of nowhere, an immediate impression makes no sense. Added to but not unified with other experiences, an
impression can give only "a feeling of complication or confusion" (*W*,
1:523), a typical effect of any partial, frustrated cognition. Mind overcomes
this mental block when it divines some sameness in a putatively novel
experience, when it recognizes a previous and familiar cognition in or
through a present impression, as in a non-French speaker encountering
homme for the first time and recognizing it by its reference to *man*. If one
were to choose the most important word in the quotation given above, it
would be not *representation* or *interpretant* but *same*, which Peirce cites
three times. Representation, represented, and interpretant all cooperate
in a general process of securing sameness, and, until this consistency is
achieved, its three elements do not exist as such. The only interpretation
that an interpretant delivers is, "This represents the same thing I represent."[8] And by that gesture it becomes an interpretant, the idea or concept

becomes represented, and the new phenomenon becomes a representation. Now the latter may be known.

Although cognition proceeds both by a category transcending the impression it categorizes and by an interpretant anterior to the impression it interprets, this double mediation does not necessarily mean that cognition exceeds the personal limits of an individual mind. It may be the case that, even though cognition occurs through hypotheses and inferences that explode the mind-object dualism, those external addresses may still be considered to be activated by or reducible to a private mental structure. James's personal consciousness may still obtain, with the representational elements of cognition encompassed by a human identity, a self-consciousness, a self, for there is no reason to suppose that a personal mind cannot subsume cognition-hypothesis-inference within its own interests and biases. Concepts and interpretants may be impersonal—only the impression is wholly personal, although it is recognized as such only by losing its uniqueness, by being understood as an instance—but in any experience they could still count only as ingredients of a mental act, their utilization determined by a mind's desire to keep itself content and intact. (At one point, Peirce calls the interpretant the "mental equivalent" of a "word or symbol" [W, 1:466].) The comparisons and differentiations that mind performs may not open mind to an otherness that breaks down mind's wholeness and privacy, that introduces an external and alienating abstraction into experience. Instead, cognition may serve merely to bring otherly data or categories under the sway of mind's already formed personality.

Cognition, then, would be not the construction or development of mind but an already constructed mind exercising, a personally complete mind extending its provenance. Cognition would be mind reaching out to objects, externalizing itself through a mental instrument whose three representational parts come together only by their unifying reference to the individual mind motivating them. James's psychological principles may remain valid despite the tripartite structure of cognition, for it may be that it is not cognition that personalizes mind but mind's personality that gives structure and meaning to cognition. Cognition may borrow on other, impersonal data and concepts for its smooth operations, but it is precisely this incorporation, this personalizing of otherness, that keeps mind privately bounded, indivisible. But, if mind is a whole thing or process within which cognition plays only a part, unless we assert the logical scandal of an effect subsuming its cause or a part explaining the whole, we must assume that some portion or act of mind remains inaccessible to cognition. If cognition obeys the directives of a personal mind, then there is no way cognition can turn around and exhaustively cognize the subjective thing directing it. Through introspection, one might say, mind can look at itself. But, in that act, mind looks at itself only as object, not as subject. Also, in order to see itself fully, mind would also have to see itself seeing, and see itself seeing itself seeing, and so on. Something of mind would always remain beyond its own cognitions. And, if that is the case, we might recall Peirce's initial question and ask, If a personal mind lies outside or remains never entirely assimilated to cognition, then how do we (or how does it) know it (or itself)? A personal, self-substantiating mind may direct cognition toward an object, but how can it become the object of its own cognitive directions? How can it know itself except as just another object of its own cognitions? In his 1872 lecture notes, Peirce wonders, "How can thought think itself, it is asked. . . . If I wish to represent to myself what my thought is, (says common sense) I have only to act as though my thought were an external object which I can consider as I should consider something not a part of myself" (*W,* 3:10). This determining private mind may in fact exist and wield knowledge as an expansive self-serving instrument, contextualizing its cognitive gestures within the purview of its personally motivated interests. But how can it be known, experienced, recognized as a personal mind (not as an object) doing all that?

What would be required here is an unmediated introspection, a direct, complete knowing of the knower. As Peirce interprets it in the first of his essays on cognition, "Questions Concerning Certain Faculties Claimed for Man," such an absolute knowledge, however, posits an "intuitive self-consciousness" that asserts not simply that cognition happens, but that it happens in a private, singular totality, an ego. The ego must turn cognition on itself and receive the ensuing knowledge as self-knowledge, as a pure introspection, a "direct perception of the internal world" (*W,* 2:206) that takes its methods entirely from the totality it originates in and returns to. Delivering not just a piece of experience, a unit of knowledge, but the unity of knowledge, introspection yields a "knowledge of the internal world not derived from external observation" (p. 206). It does not begin with some specific experience but focuses on the subjective conditions of every experience, on the personal shape of my every experience, for a genuinely personal knowledge of ourselves provides "not a mere feeling of subjective conditions of consciousness, but of our personal selves": "The self-consciousness here meant is the recognition of my *private* self. I know that *I* (not merely *the* I) exist. The question is, how do I know it? (pp. 200–201). That is the question that introspection cannot answer. Not only does Peirce's cognitive question ("how do I know?") pose the logical problem of knowing that particular individuality that lies before or behind knowing. Nor does it simply cite the methodological difficulty of "mind's watching its own operations" and realizing that it sees only "imaginary objects,—*products* of the mind's operation, but not the movement of mind itself" (*CP,* 7.376). It also signals the impossibility of knowing any particular individual particularly, since an individual is cognizable only insofar as it falls under the general category *individual* and resembles an interpretant that completes its categorization. An introspective inquiry into "who I am" can proceed only to the extent that the inquirer understands "what an I is" and can yield results only insofar as the studied "I" represents "*the* I." And that involves not simply a direct self-observation but also a judgment, an inference about the particular "I" for which the "I" itself and the introspection of it cannot entirely account. Therefore, introspection presupposes knowledge of a general "I" that contravenes the unmediated awareness of a personal "I."

With direct knowledge of the ego denied, the only reason to hypothesize its existence and activity is because it explains the consistency of experience, the unity of the manifold. Something must organize impressions and conceptions into coherent cognitions, and in the absence of any other viable solutions, a personal mind would seem to stand out as a necessary inference. Yet, although comparison, synthesis, and all other cognitive ingredients certainly imply a mind at work, it does not necessarily follow that that mind must inhabit a personal form or that personality is essential to thinking. Mind may be a necessary inference from cognition, but whether personal mindedness is a prerequisite for experience, whether personal selfhood marks *the* enabling limit of cognition, or whether there are contexts logically prior to or "subjective conditions of consciousness" more fundamental than private selfhood—those questions are, at the very least, not settled by pointing to the phenomenon of coherent experience.

So, rather than trying to answer these questions with a blank ontological statement of "the self exists and it is . . . ," Peirce once again asks about its cognizability: How (if not by introspection) do we know a private self? How and why and when do we come to infer its existence? Where does the idea of selfhood come from? These are the questions that motivate "Questions Concerning Certain Faculties Claimed for Man" and its follow-up, "Some Consequences of Four Incapacities," and that the essays proceed to answer.

Peirce first notes that cognition and self-consciousness do not arise simultaneously. Children manifest "decided intellectual activity" before they have mastered usage of the pronoun *I,* the latter incapacity indicating "an imperfect self-consciousness in them" (*W,* 2:201). Children make inferences about objects but without reflecting back on their own inference making: "No one questions that, when a sound is heard by a child, he thinks not of himself as hearing, but of the bell or other object as sounding" (p. 201). Recognizing the sound as a bell ringing, surmising that this sound is the same as sounds generally made by bells, the child performs the comparisons and predications necessary to cognition, yet this process does not require for its completion any added awareness of "I am hearing it."

So mind may have experiences without any developed idea of personal selfhood accompanying it. But, again, where or why does the idea of selfhood originate? Even though "experience is our only teacher" (*CP,* 5.50) and "every quality of which we know of is of course either experienced or inferred from experience" (*W,* 2:5), the concept of self does arise and therefore must bear some relation to some experience. That relation, as the child example shows, is not a necessary concomitant of experience, nor is it a requisite conclusion. Yet it exists, it functions. So, if experience does not provide immediately knowledge of self, then selfhood must be mediately inferred from experience. If not an object of experience, then the self must be a conceptual instrument facilitating the cognition of things. It is a useful hypothesis satisfying a cognitive need, providing a concept when mind finds its experiences difficult to comprehend. Because the "function of hypothesis is to substitute for a great series of predicates forming no unity in themselves, a single one (or small number) which involves them all" (*W,* 2:218), hypothesis happens when mind undergoes an experiential disunity and solicits a new concept, one yielding an effective synthesis of previously incomprehensible data. Hypothesis works to overcome cognitive difficulties—that is its raison d'être. A workable cognition of organized data requires no further explanation, for the concepts already called on have done their work and mind can move on in its habitual manner to other cognitions. Nothing successfully cognized throws mind back on itself or compels it to postulate a self directing it.

A novel inference of any kind, including that of selfhood, arises only when mind runs up against an incoherence, a bungled synthesis. In this case, selfhood as a unifying hypothesis originates not in some special inner cognition but through a failure of ordinary cognition, a confusion in those relations making objects and events cognizable. As Peirce describes it in a pleasantly simple parable, selfhood is a special supposition designated to account for a faulty inference: "A child hears it said that the stove is hot. But it is not, he says; and indeed, that central body [the child's body] is not touching it, and only what that touches is hot or cold. But he touches it, and finds the testimony confirmed in a striking way. Thus, he becomes aware of ignorance, and it is necessary to suppose a *self* in which this ignorance can inhere. So testimony gives the first dawning of self-consciousness" (*W,* 2:202). It is a testimony first assumed as false and then proved to be true that raises the notion of ignorance and inspires self-consciousness. It is not the experience itself but the way the experience introduces the idea of ignorance, the cognizance of a limit to cognition, that calls for a new inference. That initial mistake demands a reason, for, to cope with the painful effects of such a mistake, it is not enough simply to say that the assumption "it is not hot" is ignorant. Ignorance itself must be explained, supplied with premises that rationalize it and account for its happening. Mind may compare, differentiate, generalize the two contradictory cognitions and find one right and one wrong, but, until mind can rationalize the capacity of being right or wrong, the possibility of making cognitive mistakes, mind has no way of habituating itself to ignorance. If ignorance remains inexplicable, not placed in a rational framework, mind has no etiology for it, which is to say, mind can make no further hypotheses or inferences about it. The pains sometimes accompanying ignorance would seem random aftereffects of experience that mind has no way of anticipating or controlling, with the result that mind has no secure way of fixing belief. Ignorance needs a ground, something to orient it, to localize the experiential manifold when mind misapprehends its surroundings.

A self is where ignorance can inhere. Wrong cognitions—the recognition of which as wrong being a shock, a surprise, a doubt—can be contained inside the "central body," attributed to a partial, finite self's efforts at understanding its environs. The universe remains rational, for ignorance seems to be merely the sign of a self's incomplete education, its gradual progress toward secure beliefs, not the universe's unreasonableness. Mistakes begin to make sense. The world is no longer a totality of things comprehensible or incomprehensible but one of facts right or wrong, of inferences hazarded by a meagerly informed mind. Given objects become appearances, phenomena "either only confirmed or merely supplemented by testimony" (*W,* 2:202), so that, when a new experience contradicts a previous inference, mind knows where to place the ignorance. The contradiction remains, but the inscrutable pain of that contradiction, of having one's judgments denied by testimony, dissipates once mind locates its mistakes in a self. Indeed, by hypothesizing a self, mind can retain its emotional judgments even if they happen to be errant:

> There are those predicates which *we* [adults] know to be emotional, but which *he* [the child] distinguishes by their connection with the movements of that central person, himself (that the table wants moving, etc.) [instead of "maturely" saying "I want to move the table"]. These judgments are generally denied by others. Moreover, he has reason to think that others, also, have such judgments which are quite denied by all the rest. Thus, he adds to the conception of appearance as the actualization of fact, the conception of it as something *private* and valid only for one body. In short, *error* appears, and it can be explained only by supposing a *self* which is fallible. (p. 203)

Testimony's denial does not eradicate emotional predicates. It only limits their validity to a personal region, an exclusive location that accommodates both public error and private truth. Mind then can comprehend its errors and embrace them and so avert the alienation and futility of trying to repress or deny them. With the new concept *self* in hand, mind understands fallibility as a condition of thinking, indeed, a precondition of mental adjustment and improvement, not a wall against satisfaction or a disturbance of understanding. Supposing a fallible self provides a workable context for knowing inferences, for admitting their truth or falsity, for making sense of contradictory cognitions. Contradiction becomes knowable precisely because it is now related to a self that mistook, for, since "every cognition of which we have any conception is relative, is the cognition of a relation" (p. 177), until a self becomes constituted as a subject pole for cognitions to relate to, the relation between contradictory cognitions remains uncomprehended, inexplicable.[9] Indeed, the faulty inference does not even have the status of being an error until an errant self is supposed. Before that, there is only a blank inconsistency, an immovable opposition that mind feels as distress but does not know as erroneousness.

What mind needs to do is assign error an intellectual value. Mind must postulate a ground of comparison by which contradictory cognitions may be explained. One cognition contradicts another, but that contradiction can make sense only if it is related to something that can contain it, something larger than or outside the opposition. In itself, a contradiction is an inefficient relation, a mental agon whose terms merely collide with one another. Mind has perhaps an emotional basis for preference (e.g., "I feel less pain from this inference," or "I can comfortably agree with testimony with this one," and so on), but that does not provide mind with a logical reason for the conflict happening in the first place. To locate that reason, mind requires a greater knowledge, an explanatory concept. And that extra knowledge is not simply an addition to the previous knowledge but a delimitation of that (now) partial, entrenched knowledge. As a conception that subsumes these cognitive polarities, the idea of an inferring self comprehends any single right or wrong inference. An infallible self is a useless, contradictory formulation here, for that would entail a God's-eye view of things—"Belief that could not be false would be infallible belief and Infallibility is an Attribute of Godhead" (*Semiotic and Significs*, 72)—and that is not a view at all and explains nothing about error and ignorance except their absence. But, while a fallible self can assimilate contradiction and find grounds for correction, for choosing one cognition as correct, another as incorrect, it is crucial that mind comprehend the wrong cognition (as wrong) and not simply reject it. If mind merely overlooks the wrong cognition and follows the right cognition ("the stove is hot"), doing so because later inferences (touching the stove) bear it out, thinking remains a matter of passive conditioning, of being conducted by objects toward whatever does not cause physical or intellectual pain. While such sensation-based coercions may enter into any cognitive experience, they do not coerce mind into useful inquiry. No unification of manifold sensations or supposition of new concepts follows.

If thinking is to constitute more than a blind adaptation to new data, mind must comprehend why such changes of mind are necessary. To cope with the predicament of error, to think it through and not just repress it, mind must both select the true cognition and explain the presence of the false cognition. To do so, mind requires some contextualizing instrument that introduces truth or falsity as abiding predicates of any cognition, some concept that renders true and false cognitions discrete objects of inquiry. Even implicitly to single out one cognition as true, mind simultaneously acknowledges the possibility of a false cognition, betraying an understanding of fallibility that invests mind with corrigibility and launches a corrective inquiry into the nature of things. For that adjustment to serve as a growth of knowledge and not just a redirection of cognition, the advent of maladjustment needs to be explained, else this critical agitation stands fast as a troublesome effect whose cause remains unknown. Providing a medium within which true-false distinctions make sense, an idea of fallible selfhood ends that intellectual suffering and enables thinking to include its own mistakes in its development.

This is why, for Peirce, fallibilism signifies much more than a methodological or ethical principle of science.[10] Of course, Peirce's scientist, an antidogmatic participant in a communal inquiry, diligently acknowledges fallibilism and relinquishes any beliefs or results should the rest of the scientific community contradict them. Any other attitude would indicate an individualistic tenacity that only hinders the progress of science. But to restrict fallibility to being a postinquiry predicate consciously applied and institutionally sanctioned is to forget that any scientific ethos requires the backing of a theory of cognition, that certain "maxims of investigation . . . become necessary owing to the peculiar constitution of man in his senses, and his mental nature" (*W,* 3:35). The habit or shape of cognition determines what form inquiry will take. Scientific investigation can proceed only according to what mind can cognize (however collectively that cognition is defined). "Mental nature" determines that mind can cognize a mistaken inference only if it attributes that mistake to mind's study of objects, not to mind's object of study. Objects themselves do not change—only their reference back to an inferring self proves malleable. If mind does not refer errors to a fallible self, it can experience error only as something wrong with the object, something obstructive or nonsensical about it. But how can an object be wrong? More important, how can one think of and what can one do with a wrong object? Bearing no efficient relation to anything else, a wrong object is utterly inexplicable, which means that mind cannot do anything with it except expel it (which is not to explain it).

In hypothesizing a self that may bear the initial error, mind places itself in an inquiring attitude. In abstracting wrongness from things and then conceptualizing it as a possible predicate of thinking, not as an ontological property, mind opens reality to investigation and itself to corrigibility. Indeed, reality is a function of that investigation or of progressively exact and convergent investigations (since reality is independent of any particular person's or group's inquiries).[11] Therefore, if one wishes to explore the order of nature, to clarify ideas, to fix belief logically and scientifically, to settle opinion and reach a consensus-based reality, one must first hypothesize a fallible self. Without that hypothesis, mind cannot grasp cognitions as true or false, ignorant or informed, and so cannot learn: "The first condition of learning is to know that we are ignorant" (*W*, 3:14). Mind may experience objects as pleasurable, efficient, disturbing, and so on, but, if it wishes to inquire into the object and derive knowledge from it, mind must in part remove itself from the object's sensuous effects and begin knowing things about the object, which is to say, begin knowing that there are some things about the object that each individual mind does not know and that no particular cognition can reach. (Herein lies the pairing of doubt and inquiry that Peirce will develop at length in the "Illustrations of the Logic of Science" essays.) Knowing ignorance is precisely this distancing process, for ignorance implies an incognizance of the object's entire being and consequences, and knowing that discrepancy allows mind to occupy it strategically, thoughtfully, pragmatically. A necessary corollary to any "means of correcting our errors, or enlarging our knowledge," "the experience of ignorance . . . does enable us to experience and conceive something which is independent of our own limited views" (p. 32) but toward which our belief-fixing endeavors bring mind closer and closer.[12] Indeed, the experience of independence or exteriority is precisely what constitutes cognition as limited, as a view that can acquire a sharper focus.

If mind cannot suppose a self's error and an object's independence—again, independence of this or that cognition, not of mind in general—it can only regard its knowledge as absolute and incorrigible and then collapse in abject misunderstanding once an exorbitant object appears. Wisely, a fallible self allows at any time for the object's excessiveness and for its own partiality. Its fallibility follows from the acknowledgment that every cognition is individual and perspectival and inevitably false, for, in relation to the object's perfect reality, "there is a residuum of error in every individual's opinions" (*W*, 2:469). True, the object's complete reality coincides with inquirers' "final agreement" about it and is its ideal "destined conclusion," the limit function of collective scientific study, the objective counterpart to the "one general agreement, one catholic consent" (p. 469) toward which logical thinking constantly gravitates. But the object's wholeness and the capacity of the object to draw minds closer to a total representation of it rest on the principle that "individualism and falsity are one and the same" (*CP*, 5.402).[13] This is why the assumption of fallibility is not designed so that any individual cognition or individual mind can eliminate or overcome falsity. It is not an escape from falsity but an improvement in the comprehension of falsity that the concept of an errant self provides.

Because an individual mind not possessing a concept of fallible selfhood interprets all its knowledge as absolute, it experiences that inevitable falsity also as absolute—and paralyzing. Mind has no means of situating it, of knowing a limit of it and thereby assimilating it. But, once mind hypothesizes fallible selfhood, falsity, ignorance, and error come in relative degrees, in the sense that, say, the inference "the stove is not hot" is "more" false than is the inference "I do not think the stove is hot." Falsity becomes a comparative measurement, a fluctuating predicate assigned to inferences to a greater or lesser extent by successive inferences that falsify or verify the preceding ones. Without that relativizing of falsity (the relative level of truth is moot, unnecessary), the discrepancy between one inference and another remains absolute and incognizable. Mind would bear no unifying standard of falsity that might serve as a basis to compare them, to render them consistent (although unequal). Mind would have no extrafalsity concept to invoke on an encounter with error, to refer the falsity to and accommodate it, correct it. In assuming a fallible self, mind renders falsity a recognizable eventuality of thinking, thereby expanding mind's scope and bringing its advancing cognitions into greater accord with each other and with (scientific) testimony.

However, that hypothesis does not serve pragmatic ends if it leads to a simple subjectification of all knowledge, a blank insertion of "I think that" in front of every assertion. Knowledge may advance through the assumption of a fallible self, but that does not necessarily mean that all knowledge is determined by that self, that the self's individual interests and methods account for every conclusion. A fallible self explains error, but to take it as explaining or founding knowledge is to extend the hypothesis far beyond its original purpose and raise more problems than the one it solved. First of all, there is the ethical problem: the subjectivizing of thinking might force inquirers to admit the (at least) partial validity of every cognition, even a demonstrably wrong one. If always marked by a particular cognizer, its implications limited to a personal context of "I infer," not inference per se, a wrong cognition retains a partial truth, a private integrity as an extension of self. Truth or falsity does not even apply to such a relation, for, although a cognition may be deemed wrong under logical analysis, when related to personal motives (which, of course, are not true or false), cognitions are judged according to their usefulness to those motives. Cognitions then point not to a public realm where their relative truth might be determined by communal inquiry, but back to a private self where their correspondence to personal impulses takes precedence. To the community's judgment, the individual can always say, "I may be wrong, but I *did* think such and such and for personal reasons, and that fact no public correction can gainsay. The only way to refute me, then, is to say *I* am wrong, not just my inferences, and I cannot believe that." In effect, instead of explaining error, a concept of fallible selfhood that emphasizes the self over the fallibility tends to displace the entire issue of error and corrigibility and derail the course of public inquiry. To Peirce, this results in a "Cartesianism" that "teaches that the ultimate test of certainty is to be found in the individual consciousness" (*W*, 2:211), a teaching that fails to discriminate between what seems to be (that which one individual infers) and what really is (that which eventually every individual infers).

That distinction Cartesians ignore because they always trust to introspection to guide the formulation of their prized clear and distinct ideas (see *W*, 3:259). This raises a second, logical problem with conceiving knowledge as personally based: converting an inferred selfhood into a directly knowable, introspectable subjective ground of all inference. Just because an idea of a fallible self neatly situates faulty inferences does not mean that one can claim to know the self (not the idea of it) as an individual cause of inference in general or to witness it in the process of carrying out singular inferences. A fallible self may explain error and stand as a workable hypothesis, but to let its efficiency lead one to forget its inferential basis and allege an introspective awareness of it is to claim to get behind the initial supposition and contact the subjective thing itself. But a hypothesis is true or acceptable not because it puts mind in touch with what is hypothesized (which, then, loses its hypothetical character) but because it brings heterogeneous perceptions and cognitions into consistent relations. Enjoying an inferential, logical status, a hypothesis exists only through and for its compendiousness, the extent to which it transforms manifold data into unified experience. Overlooking a hypothesized being's explanatory footing, mind mistakenly separates that being's cognizability from its reality, pretending that the former has conducted mind to the latter and can now be dispensed with. But, while one may perhaps ignore cognitive questions when observing empirical objects, when inquiring into unobservable entities such as the self, one must ask not "What is it?" but "How is it known, how experienced?" for, given the inferential basis of even the most basic impressions, "*cognizability* (in its widest sense) and *being* are not merely metaphysically the same, but are synonymous terms" (*W,* 2:208). To assert their difference is to postulate a reality that exceeds our cognition of it. It is to conceptualize an inexperienceable existence, a concept both pragmatically superfluous (since it clarifies no ideas) and logically contradictory (since it signifies not simply a concept of otherness but the other of conceptuality, an anti- or preconceptual concept).[14]

In this case, whatever powers or priorities the concept of fallible selfhood may arrogate to the self, in fact, mind recognizes selfhood only after it commits errors and surmises a limit to its cognitive grasp. Although it signifies the source of partial suppositions, the origin of perspectival thinking, the fallible self concept remains in actuality an explanatory hypothesis, a strategic postulation out to assimilate the meaning of ignorance. It is a logical term, not a psychological essence, so the self should continue to be understood as an inference from limitation and not be aggrandized into the limit of all inference.[15] To investigate human being, inquirers should begin by clarifying the limits from which personal-mindedness springs, not by assuming a preexistent personal mind limited by external things: "In short, we can discover ourselves by those limitations which distinguish us from the absolute *ego*" (*W,* 2:162) (the latter epithet signifies the totality of thinking). A self is distinguished after the fact, set off by something beyond it, by some thing itself understood or knowable precisely through its limiting effects. A personal mind is a correlative function of two things: one is objects' other-sidedness (which only makes sense from a subject side), their resistance to internalization by any individual mind; the other is mind's condition of ignorance, its incomplete knowledge.

To take another example of Peirce's from a review of Karl Pearson's *The Grammar of Science:* "We learn there is an *ego* behind the eye" when we try to grasp "an inkstand" wholly but can do so only by approaching it from this side and that, in this way and that, developing "a generalized percept, a quasi-inference from percepts, perhaps a composite-photograph of percepts." However, because mind can always experience a new percept of or possibility in the inkstand, mind realizes that in "this psychical product is involved an element of resistance," something always left out of the picture (*CP,* 8.144). That resistance is not a physical force but a cognitive limit beyond which the total object seems to lie, with mind's efforts to surpass it producing only discrepant cognitions. Unable to make the object correspond to any single cognition of it, and likewise unable to make any cognition of it be identical to any other cognition of it, mind copes with resistance through an "inward subject-external object" hypothesis: "Subsequently, when I accept the hypothesis of an inward subject for my thoughts, I yield to that consciousness of resistance and admit the inkstand to the standing of an external object" (par. 144). This admission is designed not to prepare for some improved correspondence of cognition and object but rather to give sense to the noncorrespondence of one cognition of it and another. If one cognition of it and another ever perfectly matched up, that would be the standard to correspond to, not some proposed matching of inward subject and external object. The external object hypothetically poses an ideal goal for thinking to direct its representations toward, but, more important (and pragmatically), it serves to give consistency to an inward subject's changing cognitions. We now have a hypothesis of subjectivity and a simultaneous hypothesis of objectivity intended specifically to give rationality and congruity to successive, but slightly dissimilar, cognitions.

Now, when coupled with other comments by Peirce on the "Outward Clash," the "direct consciousness of hitting and getting hit [that] enters into all cognition" (*CP,* 8.41), "a sense of compulsion [as] an immediate knowledge of something outside the self, exerting a brute force on self" (par. 103), the language of "resistance" and "externality" suggests a noninferential, direct encounter with "a brute something without the mind" (par. 103). But what mind directly senses is imprecisely a "brute something," a barely predicated, hazy, featureless, although compelling force "without the mind." True, mind begins by apprehending "an interruption into the field of consciousness, sense of resistance, of an external fact, of another something" (*CP,* 1.377). But the latter two terms, *external fact* and *another something,* are deliberately vague, and the preposition *of* preceding them signifies an addition of knowledge to and an inference drawn from the initial moment of interruption and resistance. To describe the experience of this hitting effect as a real, external object clashing with a fallible, interested self requires several more inferential steps, and these are not falsifications or forgettings of brute experience but explanations of it (the attribution of "bruteness" being itself an inferential move).[16]

Why must the external fact be an inference? Mainly because, at first, the experience of compulsion lies not in the object but in an as yet unspecified demand for mind to think otherwise than it thought before. All experience involves cognition of objects, but the objectivity or externality of experience derives from mind's undergoing an imposed adjustment in thinking. This is why Peirce defines experience as a "forcible modification of our ways of thinking" (*CP,* 1.321), "the compulsion, the absolute constraint upon us to think otherwise than we have been thinking" (par. 336). Mind attributes that necessity to an object, surmises an external something as the cause of mind's forced alterations, and such leaps of logic amount to a hypothesis of externality. They constitute an inference that explains why cognitions conflict, why mind is pushed into a different thinking.

Again, the conflict or incongruity that compels mind to infer external objects takes place initially between one cognition and another, not between subject and object or cognizer and cognized. A shock or confusion results not simply from a new or unforeseen object or experience hitting mind from without. The qualities of newness or uncanniness arise only in relation to oldness or familiarity. An external anything can be new only if it departs from a preconception, for example, when "a man is more or less placidly *expecting* one result, and suddenly finds something in contrast to that forcing itself upon his recognition" (*CP,* 5.57). Without that old expectation, the new external is not new. Indeed, if it does not meet or disrupt or in some way relate to an expectation, the present thing remains unintelligible, unpredicated, inconceivable. What makes the new conceivable is that, although it counters the expectation, the contrast is still a relation, one that allows for an interpretation: "A duality is thus forced upon him: on the one hand, his expectation which he had been attributing to Nature, but which he is now compelled to attribute to some mere inner world, and on the other hand, a strong new phenomenon which shoves that expectation into the background and occupies its place. The old expectation, which is what he was familiar with, is his inner world, or *Ego.* The new phenomenon, the stranger, is from the exterior world, or *Non-Ego*" (par. 57). The contrast between two mental states, "expectation" and "result," a contrast that mind at first experiences as "force," yields to a "dualism" of mental and nonmental, *"Ego"* and *"Non-Ego,"* a dualism that mind can absorb as a desultory but predictable component of experience. Out of cognitive discord comes a rearrangement of the makeup of experience. An inner-inner opposition that surprises becomes an inner-outer discrepancy that can be corrected.

What that hypothesis of outer does is remove the source of bruteness and constraint from the internal workings of mind and station it in an exterior world. Just as, in order to comprehend faulty inferences, mind had to locate error in itself, in a fallible self, so in order to understand compulsion mind must locate resistance outside itself. If mind situates resistance within, if mind incorporates that force or hitting effect that can subvert any particular cognition, how can mind secure any beliefs or clarify any ideas with confidence? If thinking contains the irrational, uncontrollable cause or disturbance that thinking proposes to comprehend and regularize, then what habits can lay claim to certainty, what expectations possess sureness? Thinking can proceed only if resistance rests in what is thought, not in thinking itself. Indeed, it is impossible to conceive resistance as an element of thinking and as a rational entity or property, for how can mind think that which resists thinking and is a part of thinking? The only way for resistance to make sense is if it is external to thinking.

So, although it does not render bruteness any less compulsive, the internal self-external force description does render it knowable and rational. The hypothetical categories of self, brute, inner-outer, and so on bring each particular experience of "Outward Clash" to cognizability and meaningfulness. Even the predicate *real* is an inference designed to make being hit mean something, for the "hitting" effect is precisely what "serves to make [cognition] mean something real" (*CP,* 8.41). What else might it mean? Or, better, how else to reconcile cognitive variations with some vague compulsion to make them coincide? How else to overcome the periodic impositions that mind undergoes, the coercions that render every individual cognition inadequate and doubtful, than to suppose a real, stable object and an interpreting, desirous self? On that hypothesis, variations in cognition rest securely in the noncoincidence of the axis of vision and the axis of things. Although mind may not exactly tally the thing it hypothesizes, it has the option of altering its axis, of bringing its cognitions into better alignment with whatever compels mind to postulate an external object. Although the correspondence is never complete, mind's adjustments to the object do reduce experience's compulsory character.

Such a conclusion might seem to cast every single cognition in a skeptical light. But the hypothesis of externality counters that uncertainty, for the inferred object is whole and stable and thus offers mind an extravariable basis for comparing, testing, and assessing variable cognitions. Again, mind aims not to correspond with the object—that strategy may indeed lead to skepticism. Instead, mind works to make its successive cognitions correspond smoothly and consistently with each other. The external object postulate serves primarily to facilitate that correspondence, providing mind with an extracognitive pole to relate inconsistent cognitions to. Of course, this hypothesis requires only an idea of extracognitiveness, not a real extracognitive entity. But, whether real or ideal, it does its job: it makes inconsistency rational and corrigible. Inconsistency induces doubt, a state of cognitive paralysis, of mind fronting unsynthesized contradictory data, and, until an external object idea arrives to explain the inconsistency, mind falters. In offering mind an instrument for measuring inconsistency, the hypothesis endows mind with coherence and progress, granting mind the capacity to improve its cognitions, to learn. Although there will never be any particular cognition perfectly corresponding to the hypothesized object, out of a comparison of divergent cognitions a less errant—that is, less inconsistent—cognition shall emerge.

To extend this corrective method beyond the region of an individual mind and its diverse cognitions to a community and its diverse individuals—an analogy on which Peirce insists—an external object hypothesis asks community members to accept their partiality and join their inquiries with those of like-minded inquirers. While an individual mind unifies and compares its cognitions in an ever more accurate understanding of reality, in like manner a community unifies and compares individual minds' understandings to reach an even greater comprehension of reality. Informing the individual's and community's cognitive development is an idea of total knowledge, a point at which perception coincides with things. And the resulting vision is not a conspicuous, striking revelation but rather what everyone commonly sees and thinks. For example, even a discourse as recondite as Aristotle's can become the universal sense: because "Aristotle buil[t] upon a few deliberately chosen concepts . . . it has come to pass that Aristotelianism is babbled in every nursery, that 'English Common Sense,' for example, is thoroughly peripatetic, and that ordinary men live so completely within the house of the Stagyrite that whatever they see out of the window appears to them incomprehensible and metaphysical" (*CP*, 1.1). Such epistemic systems may mystify what lies outside them, beyond the window of their cognitive framework, but they also institute a shared method of thinking, housing individual, idiosyncratic minds in a community of inquirers and believers.

Thus, limitation serves an organizing function. Limitation, error, ignorance, resistance—all lead to the hypothesis of individual selves and independent objects, a presumptive abstraction and separation of minds from one another and from things. But, if mind remains sensitive to the hypothetical character of that process, then mind rightly holds off from converting that instrumental assumption into an ontological assertion. Specifically, mind will understand the individuation of minds into errant selves and the reconstitution of sense data into external objects as pragmatic tools, not ontological discoveries. The only significant discovery is the workability of the hypothesis, its salutary applicability to a given situation. Any pragmatic assertions about the hypothesis's content confine it in a hypothetical light, which is to say, in relation to the problems it solves. The hypothesized thing's reality, its real existence, is a separate and abstract issue.

A pragmatic mind maintains the contingent status of the object, that contingency to Peircean pragmatists being fundamentally inferential. An object (or a subject) is a hypothesis, an explanatory instrument that puts mind's ideas and experiences into consistent and rational relations with one another. To ask only "What is the being of the thing hypothesized?" is to forget the thing's hypotheticalness, to ignore what the hypothesis explains, what problem it meets, what inconsistencies it rationalizes. Pragmatic thinking interprets all things according to the specific cognitive needs that mind has at the moment.

Epilogue

Near the beginning of "How to Make Our Ideas Clear," an essay published ten years after the cognition papers appeared, Peirce records a proposition about logic that might seem to contradict his earlier fallibilistic conclusions:[1] "The very first lesson that we have a right to demand that logic shall teach us is, how to make our ideas clear; and a most important one it is, depreciated only by minds who stand in need of it. To know what we think, to be masters of our own meaning, will make a solid foundation for great and weighty thought" (*W*, 3:260). Given Peirce's contention that error and ignorance are necessary components of inquiry, we might interpret any goal of mastery over knowledge or over ourselves as a logician's or scientist's hubris. After singling out (in the previous essay, "The Fixation of Belief") scientific method as the best way to truth, Peirce seems to have forgotten the partial and incomplete nature of any particular investigation. In a way, he succumbs to the same philosophical temptation that in his eyes ruined Descartes as a methodologician: trying to reach a point of absolute certainty, of theoretical indubitability. Indeed, such "theory hope" renders Peirce liable to neopragmatism's "against theory" arguments.[2] Because the only certainty claims that Peirce can make for beliefs is that they are *practically* indubitable, the concept of any master belief or mastery over belief contradicts Peirce's basic principles of belief fixation.

But this is to misconstrue the passage cited above, for Peirce's prediction actually has a narrower theme than that indicated by the grandiose phrase "solid foundation for great and weighty thought." In Peirce's wording, the only thing mastered is meaning—not feelings, conduct, reasoning, or action. And the only thing known is what we think—not the universe or reality or history. Peirce's optimistic forecast of knowledge and control applies only to the intellectual content of our own minds. It refers, not to the control of content, but to a knowledge of that content, an awareness of what it imports. Logic aims to teach us how to make our ideas clear, how to achieve "clearness of apprehension" (*W,* 3:266), and claims to do nothing more. It does not produce or eradicate ideas—it only clarifies them. It offers no positive knowledge, no new information. Set alongside the discoveries of science, logic performs a modest analytic task, a retroactive one. It helps us know what we already think, master what we already mean. Logic attends to the mental acts that we already carry out. And, if pragmatism is a "maxim of logic," then it explicates thought and meaning and does not prescribe or evaluate them. As such, "Pragmatism makes or ought to make no pretension to throwing any positive light on any problem. It is merely a logical maxim for laying the dust of pseudoproblems" (*CP,* 8.186). "Pragmatism solves no real problems. It only shows that supposed problems are not real problems" (par. 259).[3]

Such a limited definition of pragmatism might surprise those familiar with neopragmatism, specifically, with the fact that neopragmatism "has long since given up James's somewhat restricted focus on the nature of knowledge and the meaning of truth and has turned its attention more broadly to issues that are essentially moral and political."[4] Along neopragmatic lines, pragmatism should "underwrite the radical democrat,"[5] not just sustain the disinterested logician. As West and other intellectuals would have it, pragmatism works to secure individual freedom and expand democratic process.[6] As Rorty, Fish, and others concerned about the practice of criticism would have it, pragmatism enhances practitioners' edification, their discovery of "new, better, more interesting, more fruitful ways of speaking."[7] Such reforms and edifications go to support a liberal pluralism, the rightful outcome of pragmatic inquiry. From this perspective,

Peirce's abstract proposal to know thoughts and master meanings seems like one more attempt to delay philosophy's proper involvement in political change.

It would seem correct, then, for neopragmatism to dismiss or neglect Peirce, for Peirce's circumscription of pragmatic inquiry goes along with numerous other descriptions of the analytic purposes and boundaries of pragmatic inquiry scattered throughout his canon. Repeatedly, as if to counter the extension of pragmatism beyond logical bounds, Peirce emphasizes the mission of pragmatism as a semantic method:

> What is wanted, therefore, is a method for ascertaining the real meaning of any concept, doctrine, proposition, word, or other sign. The object of a sign is one thing; its meaning is another. (*CP*, 5.6)

> I understand pragmatism to be a method of ascertaining the meanings, not of all ideas, but only of what I call "intellectual concepts," that is to say, of those upon the structure of which, arguments concerning objective fact may hinge. (par. 467)

> But pragmatism does not undertake to say in what the meanings of all signs consist, but merely to lay down a method of determining the meanings of intellectual concepts, that is, of those upon which reasonings may turn. (par. 8)

> The word *pragmatism* was invented to express a certain maxim of logic, which, as was shown at its first enouncement, involves a whole system of philosophy. The maxim is intended to furnish a method for the analysis of concepts. (*CP*, 8.191)

To Peirce, pragmatism is a method, not a morality, a conceptual explication, not a political prescription. It operates on the assumption that to know what we think is not the same as to think, that to master meaning is not the same as to mean. To think or to mean is one mental act; to understand the thought thought or the meaning meant is another mental act.[8] (Recall the distinction between having an intuition and knowing that what we are having is an intuition.) Peirce addresses solely the latter and does so, not to change the thought or meaning, but to delineate it, comprehend it. If the distinction outlined above holds, Peirce's analysis of meaning in no way involves the analysis of conduct or of the act of thinking or meaning. Such inquiries fall under the purview of ethics and psychology. In contrast, pragmatic inquiry applies only to signs and meanings and only to those signs ("any concept, doctrine, proposition, word") on which arguments and reasonings turn. And Peirce does not moralize or politicize those meanings. Rather, he details what those concepts presume and entail. In the metaphor Peirce uses to describe "the kernal of pragmaticism," pragmatic analysis reveals a concept's "valency," how it does or does not combine with other concepts: "In one respect combinations of concepts exhibit a remarkable analogy with chemical combinations; every concept having a strict valency" (*CP,* 5.469).

Peirce insists on this demarcation. Often directing his arguments against what Peirce considers James's all-too-loose conception of pragmatism (which neopragmatists favor over Peirce's), Peirce asserts that pragmatism begins as a "maxim of logic," not of conduct, politics, or ethics. Peirce would consider the Jamesian and neopragmatic extension of pragmatic analysis to real affairs invalid. However, James and neopragmatists might reply, Peirce sometimes seems to contradict his own logical stricture. In his most famous formulation, he himself connects meaning to effects and consequences, so why restrain pragmatism to conceptual explication? Indeed, the pragmatic maxim ("meaning equals consequences") encourages inquirers to extend pragmatism beyond an analysis of mind's concepts and into politic and moral critique. Given Peirce's association of meaning with effects and truth with belief, why not treat Peirce's differentiation of analyzing a concept's meaning from acting on a concept's truthfulness as precisely that which should be overcome?[9] His identification of "the whole of our conception of [an] object" with "what effects, which might conceivably have practical bearings, we conceive the object of our conception to have" (*W,* 3:266) plainly calls for a method of practical description, not logical analysis. To ignore a thing's practical influence is to impoverish our experience of it, to yield a rarefied notion of it, a formal, impersonal idea of what it is, not how it acts. Because "our idea of anything *is* our idea of its sensible effects" (p. 266), interpreting ideas as insensible abstractions is a mistake.

If these propositions are true, there seems to be no reason to confine pragmatism to some refined inspection of conceptual content (as the earlier statements asserted). Neopragmatism, then, is right to relate ideas to the practical sphere. Right pragmatic inquiry is political diagnosis, not an analysis of a concept's logical relations to other concepts, but an exposure of how a concept supports this or that individual's or group's institutional and social investments. And this is not a dismissal of meaning but a referral of meaning to its actual functional nature. In 1905, after James has popularized the pragmatic maxim, Peirce affirms: "*In order to ascertain the meaning of an intellectual conception one should consider what practical consequences might conceivably result by necessity from the truth of that conception; and the sum of these consequences will constitute the entire meaning of the conception*" (*CP*, 5.9). A concept with no consequences has no meaning. A meaning wholly abstract and ineffectual is empty—not wrong, or false, but nonsensical. Those who try to ascertain the meaning of an intellectual conception without taking a concept's practical consequences into account end up enmeshed in endless speculative disputes, disputes that cannot be solved because they are applied, not to clear notions and empirical data, but only to some fugitive, recondite entity termed *meaning*. But, while an impractical theory of meaning allows for the usual vain forensics and oblique controversies, a practical theory of meaning demands a decisive description of a concept, a detailed inventory of a concept's actual effects. Nonpragmatic theories conceive meaning as some mysterious shadow entity lying somewhere behind or above its sensible effects. The pragmatic theory draws meaning out of obscurity, makes it an affair of human practices and nothing more.

Therefore, to accept Peirce's restriction of pragmatism to logical analysis of concepts' meaning is to focus narrowly on concepts' intellectual parts. Such abstract analyses intellectualize a concept's effect and sterilize its import. It exiles a concept to formal regions, withdrawing intellect from experience, sheltering it from worldly concerns. A concept's meaning may include intellectual relations to other concepts, but those must be submitted to a larger context of practical benefits, belief fixation, personal satisfaction, and so on. Only then will we know what we think and master what we mean.

This interpretation seems inescapable, for Peirce's insistence on the essential role of consequences in the determination of meaning is unambiguous. On this principle, Peirce's arguments fully support the antitheory stand taken by neopragmatists. However, granting the distinction between an analysis of a concept's intellectual relations and an analysis of its practical consequences, allowing that there is a significant difference between logical dissection and practical description, should we conclude along with neopragmatists that the consequences and effects Peirce talks about are as actual and real and alogical as the interpretation outlined above would suggest? Does Peirce's pragmatic maxim refer to any and all consequences? Roughly speaking, the neopragmatic interpretation defines practical consequences as whatever historical or political changes follow from belief in the concept. But is there no finer discrimination to be made regarding the term *consequences* that might give pragmatism some purview separate from political or historical approaches to consequences?

Such a distinction is, indeed, to be found in the very maxim quoted above. In Peirce's phrasing, the pragmatic semantics of a conception address only those practical consequences that "*might conceivably result by necessity from the truth of that conception.*" The terms *conceivably* and *necessity* here mark a crucial subdivision of inquiry, one that distinguishes the object of pragmatic analysis from that of political, ideological, and historical questioning. It is not any result that happens but only the necessary results of which one can conceive, on which pragmatic inquiry focuses. Necessity implies a logical connection between concept and consequence, not a historical or an ideological one, so the pragmatist speaks of consequences only in conditional terms (what would happen), not in actual terms (what did happen). Of course, a particular result may indicate that historical or ideological conditions were determining factors in the event, but, just as those conditions constantly change, so do the results they condition. Those conditions and outcomes certainly exist, but they involve too many accidental variables and local circumstances to fall within the province of pragmatic analysis. Pragmatism (in Peirce) cares not for this inquirer's mental disposition or that inquirer's cultural conditioning, along with all the knowledge products framed by those determinants. Instead, pragmatism seeks the shortest route to those aspects of an inquiry's conclusions that are necessary. Many aspects will be entirely contingent on local circumstances, but those are not the object of pragmatic analysis. Focusing exclusively on necessary relations, those whose negation is a logical contradiction, pragmatism searches after consequences that particular historical conditions and individual inclinations cannot alter.

That is why, in his methodological pragmatic statements about meaning, Peirce underscores the hypothetical, conditional, conceptual nature of consequences or conduct or action. The practical considerations for which he wishes to account and to which he wishes to relate meaning are always surrounded by such terms as *conceivable, concept of, an idea of, would be, would happen, suppose,* and *consider* (as imperatives), terms emphasizing, not experience and action themselves, but our conceptualization of them:

> I deny that pragmaticism as originally defined by me made the intellectual purport of symbols to consist in our conduct. On the contrary, I was most careful to say that it consists in our *concept* of what our conduct *would* be upon *conceivable* occasions. (*CP,* 8.208)

> It is only of *conceptions,* that is, of the intellectual part of meaning that I was speaking. The pragmaticist need not deny that such ideas as those of action, of actual happening, of individuality, of existence, etc., involve something like a reminiscence of an exertion of brute force which is decidedly anti-intellectual, which is an all-important ingredient of the practical, although the pragmat[ic]istic interpretation leaves it out of account. Yet while he may admit that this idea of brute thereness,—or whatever best names it,—is quite distinct from any concept, yet he is bound to maintain that this does not suffice to make an idea of practical reality. (par. 195; here Peirce is speaking in the voice of the pragmaticist)

This is a methodological demarcation, for while the pragmatist grants that "conduct," "action," and any other "actual happening," understood as "ideas," do relate in some dim, "reminiscent" way to "brute force," pragmatic analysis simply skirts them. It fastens on "the intellectual part of meaning." Although meaning involves conduct and consequences, only their "*conceivable* occasion" forms pragmatism's subject matter. "Intellectual purport," the object of pragmatic study, does not rest in the actual events themselves or in the "brute force" that putatively constitutes the practical world. Indeed, although an "ingredient" of practical reality, "brute force" alone cannot provide an "idea of practical reality." To know practical reality and to cognize the brute force shaping it requires a concept that differs from the experienced force. This concept is the focus of pragmatic definition.

The question is, Must we retain Peirce's focus on hypothetical consequences, or may we simply move on to neopragmatism's real consequences? Why chase an idea of practical reality and not real practices? Why explore a concept of conduct's conceivable occasion and not address actual occasions of conduct? The answer to these questions lies in the inferential model of cognition presupposed by Peirce's pragmatic method. First, particular instances of a practical reality or conduct do not fully explain those instances' occurrence. Second, in order to carry out an investigation of human events and ascertain the ingredients of the world of practice, inquiry must invoke terms of explanation, ideas that, although relevant to the event analyzed, cannot be derived from the event. The exploration needs conceptual tools with which to explore the event, and these the event in its practical aspect cannot provide. So any pragmatic analysis must acknowledge these abstract elements. Third, and most important, the cognition of the consequence rests not only on the presence of the consequence to the sense but also on an idea of what it is, an awareness of what it is like and not like. These are part of the consequence's cognizability. Before a consequence can even be recognized as an actual occurrence, mind must possess some conception of the consequence as something presentable to sense and submissible to interpretation.

Peirce's cognition writings of the 1860s made this clear: the prerequisite for comprehending a phenomenon is its comparability to other phenomena, and the basis of comparison is itself not a phenomenon but an idea. The phenomenon's intelligibility lies not in the phenomenon itself but in its being related to other phenomena, the first relation here being that they all fall into the class *phenomena*. To understand the meaning of a concept, we examine what practical consequences follow from its truth. Here, Peirce and neopragmatism agree. But to understand those consequences, not only must we execute a practical description of them, but we must also analyze the consequences' consistency, their relatedness to other phenomena. This consistency is the basis of consequences' meaning, the trait that lets them be cognized and changed.

Neopragmatism overlooks this intelligibility requirement. Consequently, its moral-political pragmatic method is incomplete. Neopragmatic analyses of ideas and events may reveal their moral and political parameters, but they generally ignore a crucial element of ideas' and events' significance: their cognizability. To fill out the understanding of consequences, we attend to how they are cognized, and in so doing we add to the pragmatic maxim ("Consider what effects . . . ") a concept of pragmatic mind. The maxim ostensibly leads inquiry away from concepts, classes, ideas, and other abstractions and toward practice, conduct, actual events, and local circumstances. In pragmatic contexts, however, a consequential happening is not just an isolated piece of practical reality, a raw occurrence fully explicable in terms of its existential content. Such consequences may be studied in wholly existential or even political terms. But, for any particular consequence to be experienced as a consequence, it must possess some features leading it to be experienced as such, and some of those features are not unique to that particular consequence. To cognize them as effects, mind first recognizes them as manifestations of some general idea, instantiations of some category, those categories and ideas serving as cognitive tools bringing the consequences to intelligibility.

Hence, turning attention from concept to consequence does not mean that pragmatists ask simply, "What are the consequences?" Neopragmatists often speak of consequences and contingencies as historical, social, or political events[10] or merely as instances of "institutional nesting."[11] But consequences do not just appear before our eyes as bits of historical reality. Consequences are historical, but their historical particularity is not their entire reality. In recognizing consequences, in inquiring into and revising them, pragmatists make inferences about them that go beyond their presence to the senses. To recognize those inferences, inquirers must also ask, "How do we know these consequences? What is the basis of these consequences' cognizability?" A wholly noncognitive inquiry reveals the historical causes and political interests lying behind consequences, but it does not touch the beliefs, habits, and concepts that are also lying behind consequences and that neopragmatists themselves acknowledge. To reach the latter, pragmatists need an understanding of consequences that incorporates concepts, not just conduct and institutions—precisely what Peirce provides with his cognition-based approach. Because cognition is inference based (contra intuition), any consequence is cognizable only if it is consistent with other phenomena and the consistency lies in class concepts and categorical distinctions, not in what is given in the phenomenon. So, when pragmatic inquiry focuses on practical consequences, it does so to flesh out the relations that make the consequences conceivable, experienceable.

Since no particular consequence can contain its own consistency and, hence, its intelligibility, practical description can never fully explain a consequence. Although methods of observation may enumerate the properties and probabilities of the consequence's occurrence, they cannot explain the togetherness of the phenomena in that occurrence, their being cognized as orderly and coherent participants in a consequential moment. Practical analysis interprets that unity in terms of spatial and temporal proximity—phenomena appearing side by side or second to second— relations that may imply the phenomena's probable reoccurrence together but that do not account for the parts' cognizability as unified, not merely juxtaposed. Therefore, in analyzing practical consequences, pragmatic inquirers must address those things that make consequences cognizable: namely, the "general ideas" that unify phenomena into a consequential whole and then put that whole into regular and consistent relations with other consequences. In an entry on "pragmatic and pragmatism" for J. M. Baldwin's *Dictionary of Philosophy and Psychology* (1902), Peirce writes: "If it be admitted, on the contrary, that action wants an end, and that that end must be something of a general description, then the spirit of the maxim itself, which is that we must look to the upshot of our concepts in order rightly to apprehend them, would direct us towards something different from practical facts, namely, to general ideas, as the true interpreters of our thought" (*CP*, 5.3).

The maxim that neopragmatists take as anti-intellectual in fact directs us toward the ideas that it supposedly practicalizes and deidealizes. The local contingencies that pragmatic assumptions are often thought to highlight give way here to a general description, an interpretation of the specific practical fact as an instance of some general law. This is not to say that Peirce's analysis is theoretical, that it seeks a general law outside all practical contexts. In Peirce's thinking, that law is not some abstract formula but indeed the practice in its habitual usage, "for every habit has, or is, a general law" (*CP*, 2.148). But to cognize the practice, to understand a consequence as an example of this or that practice, requires a concept of the practice as such. No particular action or conduct that we may interpret as an instance of the practice can account for its instantiation. Because a consequence's capacity of being an instance is necessary to its cognizability (knowing something is always knowing it *as*), pragmatic analysis analyzes precisely those concepts that instantiate it, for, while a consequence marks a specific practical result, its comprehension by inquirers requires that it fit some generalization, that it be capable of "regularization." In a letter to James, Peirce admits, "That everything is to be tested by its practical results was the great text of my early papers." But, he goes on to say, "I have seen more thoroughly than I used to do that it is not mere action as brute exercise of strength that is the purpose of all, but say generalization, such action as tends toward regularization" (*CP,* 8.250).

This distinction between brute exercise and generalization indicates why Peirce's spotlight on practical considerations appears first in an essay entitled "How to Make Our Ideas Clear" and why the intellectual aim subsumes the practical emphasis. Pragmatism turns to outcomes (again, conditional ones, not real ones; what would happen, not what did happen) in order to explicate ideas. But those ideas are the things that make sense out of outcomes, that regularize them, that put them into relations that make them cognizable. This *is* generalization. Of course, generalizing ideas are not all that is contained in an outcome, for no outcome can be conceived as existing outside some specific historical context and having no phenomenal content. It has to occur at some time and in some place and to be "sensible." Itemizing those sensible particulars is a crucial empirical procedure, but one yielding only a partial understanding of the consequence. Particulars alone cannot evoke the regularity that runs through this consequence and that one, that makes it fall into this or that category. Sensible particulars singularize a consequence, make it discrete. But an absolutely singular consequence, a consequence with no relation to anything else, would not even be singular, for singularity is itself a generalization. A purely unique consequence, one not *classified* as unique or pure or consequential, one receiving no categorizing attribution whatsoever, would not be recognizable as anything, would not be recognizable. A concept is requisite, and this is precisely why concepts have sensible effects.

Hence Peirce's insistence that his pragmatic maxim "is intended to furnish a method for the analysis of concepts" (*CP,* 8.191). That method is an essential component in the understanding of consequences. The consequences may be partly described in political or objective terms, in accordance with the neopragmatic interpretation of consequences. But a complete analysis of the reality of consequences soon throws inquirers back on the concepts bringing consequences to intelligibility. As we have seen, unless one wishes to posit an incognizable reality, which is to say, to claim to cognize it (as incognizable), one must agree that "*cognizability* (in its widest sense) and *being* are not merely metaphysically the same, but are synonymous terms" (*W,* 2:208). Of course, neopragmatists agree with this connection of being and cognizability, for a separation of the two assumes an inaccessible, transhistorical, apolitical region of being, precisely the opposite world of neopragmatic concentration—politics, institutions, concrete life. So it makes no sense for neopragmatists to ignore the cognition criterion in their focus on consequences. Indeed, in this shift from being to cognizability, Peirce supplies inquirers, including neopragmatists, with a sound validation for taking the first pragmatic step: abandoning a correspondence theory of truth.

As we have seen (in the preface), neopragmatism requires anticorrespondence in order to sanction pragmatic adjustments in how we understand and live in the world.[12] But neopragmatism typically backs up its affirmations not with arguments but with blank assertions of antifoundationalism or antiessentialism ("we should not try to ground our beliefs in an extrahuman reality") or with political imperatives ("we should be liberal pluralists"). Peirce's conclusion that analyzing a consequence's being implies analyzing its cognizability provides just this justification. This is why pragmatists should hearken to Peirce's early cognition papers, where he develops a distinct concept of mind to which he adheres in his later writings, including those on pragmatic method. That concept and its concomitant model of cognition rest on a few unshakable premises, one of which is that the cognition of any object, action, or consequence is the cognition of its relations. Another is that those relations do not themselves constitute objects, actions, or consequences but instead import a concept, a class, a category. In the light of these premises, the terms of pragmatic method that neopragmatists have interpreted as naming real, concrete existences—*practical consequences, sensible effect, conduct, habit*—in truth have a conceptual basis. That basis and the cognitive services that it provides are the proper object of pragmatic inquiry.

Of course, many other kinds of inquiry can and should proceed. The practical phenomena that Peirce foregrounds rightfully undergo empirical description, ethical judgment, probabilistic calculation, and so on. But pragmatism reserves for itself the conceivability of phenomena. In focusing not on an individual cognition of this or that phenomenon but on this or that phenomenon's cognizability, the general conditions of its being cognized, Peirce's pragmatism singles out its own conceptual domain. The inferential theory of cognition, specifically, its hypothesis that every cognition involves the inference of a particular's relatedness, of how it has the character of . . . , or is an instance of . . . , or bears the attributes of . . . , makes concepts into essential constituents of understanding, even at the level of sensation. They are not the only constituents, for in any event of cognition physical properties like the physiology of the senses and historical circumstances like the cognizer's age, nationality, and language participate. To explicate the concepts involved, the pragmatic inquirer appeals to these contingent factors. But the pragmatist maintains that these functional concepts cannot be reduced to the cognized data in their historical appearance. This conceptual dimension is a function of pragmatic mind and the field of pragmatic analysis. This is the focus of pragmatic method.

Notes

Preface: Pragmatism and Criticism

1 Richard Rorty, *Philosophy and the Mirror of Nature* (Princeton, N.J.: Princeton University Press, 1979). The anthology is *Against Theory: Literary Studies and the New Pragmatism,* ed. W. J. T. Mitchell (Chicago: University of Chicago Press, 1985).

2 Richard Rorty, *Consequences of Pragmatism* (Minneapolis: University of Minnesota Press, 1982), 160.

3 Besides his *Philosophy and the Mirror of Nature* and *Consequences of Pragmatism,* see also Richard Rorty's *Contingency, Irony, and Solidarity* (Cambridge: Cambridge University Press, 1989), *Objectivity, Relativism, and Truth* (Cambridge: Cambridge University Press, 1991), and *Essays on Heidegger and Others* (Cambridge: Cambridge University Press, 1991); Walter Benn Michaels, "The Interpreter's Self: Peirce on the Cartesian 'Subject,' " in *Reader Response Criticism: From Formalism to Post-Structuralism,* ed. Jane Tompkins (Baltimore: Johns Hopkins University Press, 1980), 185–200; Frank Lentricchia, *Ariel and the Police: Michel Foucault, William James, Wallace Stevens* (Madison: University of Wisconsin Press, 1988); Giles Gunn, *Thinking across the American Grain: Ideology, Intellect, and the New Pragmatism* (Chicago: University of Chicago Press, 1992); Cornel West, *The American Evasion of Philosophy: A Genealogy of Pragmatism* (Madison: University of Wisconsin Press, 1989).

4 Rorty, *Consequences of Pragmatism,* xiii.

5 Stanley Fish, *Is There a Text in This Class? The Authority of Interpretive Com-*

munities (Cambridge, Mass.: Harvard University Press, 1980), 370–71, and "Consequences," in *Against Theory*, 123–28; Steven Knapp and Walter Benn Michaels, "Against Theory," in ibid., 104–5.

6 Rorty, *Consequences of Pragmatism*, 167.

7 Knapp and Michaels, "Against Theory," 30.

8 Rorty, *Consequences of Pragmatism*, xix.

9 Rorty, *Objectivity, Relativism, and Truth*, 13.

10 Fish, "Consequences," 111.

11 See Knapp and Michaels, "Against Theory," 21–24.

12 Harold Bloom, *Agon: Towards a Theory of Revisionism* (New York: Oxford University Press, 1982), 39.

13 Richard Rorty, "Philosophy without Principles," in *Against Theory*, 135.

14 Rorty, *Contingency, Irony, and Solidarity*, 44.

15 West, *The American Evasion of Philosophy*, 239.

16 Rorty, *Contingency, Irony, and Solidarity*, xiv.

17 Frank Lentricchia, *Criticism and Social Change* (Chicago: University of Chicago Press, 1983), 11.

18 Lentricchia, *Ariel and the Police*; West, *The American Evasion of Philosophy*, 206; Gunn, *Thinking across the American Grain*, 112.

19 See Ross Posnock, "Before and After Identity Politics," *Raritan* 15 (1995): 95–115.

20 West, *The American Evasion of Philosophy*, 210.

21 Richard Rorty, "The Banality of Pragmatism and the Poetry of Justice," *Southern California Law Review* 63 (1990): 1911.

22 Rorty, *Philosophy and the Mirror of Nature*, 155–64, 389–94.

23 West, *The American Evasion of Philosophy*, 6, 209, 5.

24 Ross Posnock, "The Politics of Pragmatism and the Fortunes of the Public Intellectual," *American Literary History* 3 (1991): 584.

25 Gunn, *Thinking across the American Grain*, 115–16.

Introduction

1 Rudolf Carnap, "Empiricism, Semantics, and Ontology," reprinted in *Meaning and Necessity: A Study in Semantics and Modal Logic* (Chicago: University of Chicago Press, 1956), 214.

2 Willard V. O. Quine, *Word and Object* (Cambridge, Mass.: MIT Press, 1960), 275.

3 Herbert W. Schneider, *A History of American Philosophy*, 2d ed. (New York: Columbia University Press, 1963); Bruce Kuklick, *The Rise of American Philosophy: Cambridge, Massachusetts, 1860–1930* (New Haven, Conn.: Yale Univer-

sity Press, 1977); Elizabeth Flower and Murray Murphey, *A History of Philosophy in America,* 2 vols. (New York: Capricorn/Putnam's, 1977); and H. S. Thayer, *Meaning and Action: A Critical History of Pragmatism* (Indianapolis: Hackett, 1981). For recent surveys of pragmatism, see Cornel West, *The American Evasion of Philosophy;* John Smith, *America's Philosophical Vision* (Chicago: University of Chicago Press, 1992); John Patrick Diggins, *The Promise of Pragmatism: Modernism and the Crisis of Authority* (Chicago: University of Chicago Press, 1992); and James Livingston, *Pragmatism and the Political Economy of Cultural Revolution, 1850–1940* (Chapel Hill: University of North Carolina Press, 1994).

1 Thinking in the Emersonian Way

1 For studies of classic American Renaissance scholarship focusing on this Emersonian problematic of self-nature-tradition, see Walter Benn Michaels and Donald E. Pease, eds., *The American Renaissance Reconsidered* (Baltimore: Johns Hopkins University Press, 1985); Russell Reising, *The Unusable Past: Theory and the Study of American Literature* (New York: Methuen, 1986); Donald E. Pease, *Visionary Compacts: American Renaissance Writings in Cultural Context* (Madison: University of Wisconsin Press, 1987); Peter C. Carafiol, *The American Ideal: Literary History as a Worldly Activity* (New York: Oxford University Press, 1991); and Morris Dickstein, *Double Agent: The Critic and Society* (New York: Oxford University Press, 1992).

2 All quotations from Emerson are taken from one of the following two editions: *The Complete Works of Ralph Waldo Emerson* (cited as *W*), ed. Edward W. Emerson, 14 vols. (Boston: Houghton Mifflin, 1903–4); *The Collected Works of Ralph Waldo Emerson* (cited as *CW*), ed. Robert E. Spiller et al., 5 vols. (Cambridge, Mass.: Harvard University Press, 1971–).

3 While much of the best American Renaissance scholarship is devoted to studying the historical and social complexities of the Emersonian debate with history and society, my interest is not primarily in how this philosophical event functions as a historical event. Rather, the aims of this analysis accord with a statement David Marr makes in *American Worlds since Emerson* (Amherst: University of Massachusetts Press, 1988): "There is a literary-philosophical narrative of Emersonianism to be written" (p. 9). That story, Marr claims, need not be related only in a social history of American life but can also be explored in a "history . . . of forgotten or unacknowledged patterns of thought and feeling" (p. 6).

4 For sophisticated readings along these lines, see Sacvan Bercovitch, "Emerson, Individualism, and Liberalism," in *The Rites of Assent: Transformations in the*

Symbolic Construction of America (New York: Routledge, 1993), 307–52; Olaf Hansen, *Aesthetic Individualism and Practical Intellect: American Allegory in Emerson, Thoreau, Adams, and James* (Princeton, N.J.: Princeton University Press, 1990); Quentin Anderson, *Making Americans: An Essay on Individualism and Money* (New York: Harcourt Brace Jovanovich, 1992); and Christopher Newfield, *The Emerson Effect: Individualism and Submission in America* (Chicago: University of Chicago Press, 1996). A recent study of Emerson that relates individualism to some of the pragmatic issues raised here is David M. Robinson's *Emerson and the Conduct of Life: Pragmatism and Ethical Purpose in the Later Work* (Cambridge: Cambridge University Press, 1993). Robinson proposes to focus on "the pragmatic Emerson" who "is the social Emerson, best regarded as a moral or ethical philosopher who was beginning to see and assess the impact of larger social transformations on the moral life of the individual" (p. 6). Robinson goes on to outline the development of a "complete moral theory" (p. 21) in Emerson's later essays, a development marking a shift from the interpretation of "visionary ecstasy as a reliable religious foundation" to a "gradual orientation toward ethical engagement as a means of spiritual fulfillment" (p. 3). Robinson identifies the latter attitude as a "pragmatic orientation" (p. 3), a connection that simplistically equates pragmatism with a humanist ethics, a blank "elevation of the practical over the theoretical" (p. 62).

Another recent work placing the idea of individualism in a pragmatic context but avoiding the above oversimplification is David Jacobson's *Emerson's Pragmatic Vision: The Dance "of" the Eye* (University Park: Pennsylvania State University Press, 1993). Although Jacobson likewise uses the term *pragmatism* without defining it specifically or relating it to Peirce's or James's notions (neither writer is cited), his argument remains consistent with a narrow philosophical understanding of the term. Jacobson does not try to broaden the meaning of *pragmatism* into social or ethical spheres. Remaining mindful of the possible conflicts between pragmatism and humanism, thinking and individuality, law and will, Jacobson recognizes that such connections require arguments and evidence that extend well beyond the limits imposed by a critical study of but one writer, even one as prodigious as is Emerson.

5 Emerson speaks here on "*man's* condition," but, hoping to downplay the strict association of "theory," "thinking," and so on with masculinity, I have opted to use the words *mind* or *individual* instead of *man*. This is a tenuous revision and raises the question whether "degenderizing" Emerson's language is philologically valid. Two texts that broadly address the issue of Emerson's gender determinations are Erik Ingvar Thurin's *Emerson as Priest of Pan: A Study in the Metaphysics of Sex* (Lawrence: Regents Press of Kansas, 1981), an erudite historical survey of gender discourses (Plato, Plutarch, Ovid, Milton, and others)

informing Emerson's arguments; and Eric Cheyfitz's *The Trans-Parent: Sexual Politics in the Language of Emerson* (Baltimore: Johns Hopkins University Press, 1981).

Another examination of Emerson and gender is to be found in David Leverenz, *Manhood and the American Renaissance* (Ithaca, N.Y.: Cornell University Press, 1989), which contains a chapter entitled "The Politics of Emerson's Man-Making Words." Leverenz's argument contends that Emerson transformed "the desperate competitiveness" of his society by "develop[ing] a style of imperious nonchalance, a manliness beyond any competition." But still, he says, "though Emerson challenges the social definitions of manhood and power, he doesn't question the more fundamental code that binds manhood and power together at the expense of intimacy," a code that ultimately "eras[es] female subjectivity" (p. 44). Hence, the "power" that Emerson worships as a transindividual force of life retains a "male" character.

6 Emerson's assertion parallels in idea and intent (to counter skepticism) Wittgenstein's aphorisms on questions and answers in the *Tractatus Logico-Philosophicus* (London: Routledge & Kegan Paul, 1922). Wittgenstein writes, "If a question can be put at all, then it *can* also be answered. . . . For doubt can only exist where there is a question; a question only where there is an answer, and this only where something *can* be *said*" (p. 187). This kind of philosophical connection between Emerson and Wittgenstein has been drawn out in a series of eccentric but captivating readings by Stanley Cavell, who finds that each thinker "pictures" thinking in analogous and remarkably fruitful ways. See Stanley Cavell, "Thinking of Emerson," a section added to *The Senses of Walden* (San Francisco: North Point Press, 1980), *In Quest of the Ordinary: Lines of Scepticism and Romanticism* (Chicago: University of Chicago Press, 1988), *This New yet Unapproachable America: Lectures after Emerson after Wittgenstein* (Albuquerque, N. Mex.: Living Batch Press, 1989), and *Conditions Handsome and Unhandsome: The Constitution of Emersonian Perfectionism* (Chicago: University of Chicago Press, 1990).

7 For a reading of this passage that singles out the importance of "theory" in *Nature,* see Julie Ellison, *Emerson's Romantic Style* (Princeton, N.J.: Princeton University Press, 1984). Ellison claims that "*Nature* is an investigation of theory" idolizing "the figure of Emerson's theorist, who is the hero . . . by virtue of his critique of origins, analogies, causes, and effects" (p. 85).

8 For an extended discussion of Emerson and reification, see Carolyn Porter, *Seeing and Being: The Plight of the Participant Observer in Emerson, James, Adams, and Faulkner* (Middletown, Conn.: Wesleyan University Press, 1981), 91–118. Porter uses Lukacs's analysis of reification and class consciousness as a model for describing mid-nineteenth-century America's progress into advanced cap-

italism. Porter regards Emerson's project as an intervention into the objectification and commodification of "sensuous human activity." A brief, but insightful, reading of Emerson and commodification in a strictly commercial context is to be found in Michael T. Gilmore, *American Romanticism and the Marketplace* (Chicago: University of Chicago Press, 1985), 18–34.

9 In *The House of Emerson* (Lincoln: University of Nebraska Press, 1982), Leonard Neufeldt has skillfully charted Emerson's understanding of "thinking" as an "epistemological ascent" (p. 26), the rule of process being "metamorphosis" (see pp. 25–46). For a comprehensive exposition of the philosophical backgrounds of Emerson's thinking, see David Van Leer, *Emerson's Epistemology: The Argument of the Essays* (Cambridge: Cambridge University Press, 1986). Van Leer struggles to sort out the Platonic, Cartesian, Humean, Swedenborgian, and, most important, Kantian thematics shaping Emerson's ideas, however much Emerson may be assimilating and distorting them.

10 Van Leer (*Emerson's Epistemology,* 50–52) argues that, for Emerson, empiricism is the frame within which perceptions have their given place. Subjectivity may transcend or comprehend this frame, but the empirical world of sensation is necessary to the life of that subjectivity. John Michael (*Emerson and Skepticism: The Cipher of the World* [Baltimore: Johns Hopkins University Press, 1988]) performs a dense but lucid articulation of Emerson's position on the skeptical implication of empiricism. Michael's analysis of Hume's influence on Emerson's "noble doubt" (pp. 36–64) clearly illuminates the essays' wavering positions on skepticism and belief, especially considering the difficult distinction that Emerson makes between "good" skepticism (Montaigne's) and "bad" skepticism (Pyrrhonism) in his essay on Montaigne. For an extensive analysis of Emerson's early struggles with Humean thought, see Evelyn Barish, *Emerson: The Roots of Prophecy* (Princeton, N.J.: Princeton University Press, 1989), 99–115.

11 Ellison (*Emerson's Romantic Style*) notes how "antagonism" becomes both a principle of Emerson's rhetoric (pp. 12–14) and a characteristic of "theory" (p. 95).

12 *Correspondence* is a loaded term in Emerson's vocabulary. Here, it simply means the traditional correspondence theory of truth, not that typological or Swedenborgian notion of correspondence from which Emerson borrows to articulate his metaphysics of nature. For a treatment of the latter, see B. L. Packer, *Emerson's Fall: A New Interpretation of the Major Essays* (New York: Continuum, 1982), 32–41. The point is not that Emerson does not believe in correspondence hypotheses or tests of truth but rather that, to the sage, correspondence should be an event in itself, or something that simultaneously happens with an event, and not an abstract predication about an event or a pre- or postsupposition in reference to it.

13 Friedrich Nietzsche, *The Will to Power*, trans. Walter Kaufmann and R. J. Hollingdale, ed. Walter Kaufmann (New York: Random House, 1967), 291.

14 Lawrence Rosenwald, *Emerson and the Art of the Diary* (New York: Oxford University Press, 1988), 142.

15 Openness is the fundamental law of culture because it is the highest attribute of experience. Gertrude Reif Hughes writes that "experience functions for Emerson as it does in Saint Paul's letter to the Romans; it is the cause of a hope that need not make for shame, because it is the result of an openness (Saint Paul calls it 'patience') that is tempered rather than weakened by tribulation" (*Emerson's Demanding Optimism* [Baton Rouge: Louisiana State University Press, 1984], xi). *Surprise* is perhaps the name for the kind of experience that openness can yield.

16 The phrase "whole centrifugal progression" comes from Alan Hodder, *Emerson's Rhetoric of Revelation: "Nature," the Reader, and the Apocalypse Within* (University Park: Pennsylvania State University Press, 1989), 80.

17 For one example of a political reading along these lines, see David Simpson, *The Politics of American English, 1776–1850* (New York: Oxford University Press, 1986), 230–59, which hastily draws out some of the "hegemonic" implications of Emerson's (and other transcendentalists') theory of language. For an erudite discussion of Emerson's politics (broadly understood), see Marr, *American Worlds since Emerson*, 40–72.

18 Such challenges to epistemological authorities constitute the task of the skeptic. But the skeptic criticizes social tendencies not in order to destabilize society but in order to regenerate it. The skeptic is out to preserve, as Michael writes, "the endless confrontation of the inner self—its thoughts, memories, beliefs, and identity—with a thousand-eyed and monstrous public that encircles it and upon whose judgment it relies" (*Emerson and Skepticism*, 139). "Man or woman thinking" decays when either combatant prevails, when the individual and its society mitigate their mutual antagonism. Skepticism maintains the tension of public and private. In Jacobson's more epistemological language, "Skeptical judgment settles self-reliance in the context of a phenomenological method that relies on acts of unconditioned will to illuminate the relations in one's world," which in turn "suggests the reciprocity of thought and action, sight and will" (*Emerson's Pragmatic Vision*, 38).

19 For explications of Emerson's own oscillating arguments and ambiguous rhetoric, see Hughes, *Emerson's Demanding Optimism*, 1–18; Packer, *Emerson's Fall*, 1–21; and Ellison, *Emerson's Romantic Style*, 75–84.

20 Readings of this somewhat infrequently commented-on essay may be found in Michael, *Emerson and Skepticism*, 155–58; Neufeldt, *The House of Emerson*, 207–11; Hodder, *Emerson's Rhetoric of Revelation*, 83–84; David Robinson,

" 'The Method of Nature' and Emerson's Period of Crisis," in *Emerson Centenary Essays,* ed. Joel Myerson (Carbondale: Southern Illinois University Press, 1982), 74–92; and Jacobson, *Emerson's Pragmatic Vision,* 91–114. Hodder focuses primarily on *Nature,* but, when discussing Emerson's "mechanics of inspiration," he looks to "The Method of Nature" for analogies of human creativity. What he finds is, of course, the "resistless torrent" and "dizzy flux" articulated in the essay. But Hodder finds a point of stability there: specifically, "nature's eternal contact with its inexhaustible power source" (pp. 82–83). But although Emerson often posits some such fixity, other assertions of his suggest that *any* fixity is a conservation, a constraint on the flux of nature. Those resistances may be necessary to human life (a theme that Nietzsche will pick up fifty years later), but they still constitute a defense against the disorienting implications of "perpetual inchoation." Although Robinson's reading sets up a biographical context for reading the essay, it then turns to the question of how "The Method of Nature" "posits an ongoing process of expression" (p. 80), "the endless process of emanation itself" (p. 83). For Robinson, this focus compels Emerson to reformulate his moral philosophy, but this turn to a radical notion of *transformation* is actually a logical consequence of the epistemology of *Nature.* Jacobson implies the latter when he interprets "The Method of Nature" as the pivotal essay in which Emerson turns from humanism to antihumanism. Jacobson's Heideggerean analysis finds Emerson asserting in "The Method of Nature" "the superficiality of individual thinking," "superficiality" being due to nature's perpetual withdrawal from any particular human experience of it: "Emerson still views Man as the expressive, phenomenological power in nature, the will that articulates the presence of nature. But he indicates that power is settled in what is withheld from speech: settled, therefore, in nature understood as the dynamic of a revealing activity that withholds itself in the very act of self-revelation" (p. 99).

21 Packer, *Emerson's Fall,* 195.
22 Wittgenstein, *Tractatus,* 187.

2   William James's Psychology of Pragmatic Thinking

 1 Henry James, *Hawthorne* (New York: AMS, 1968), 42.
 2 Henry James, *Letters,* ed. Leon Edel, 4 vols. (Cambridge, Mass.: Harvard University Press, 1974–84), 2:274.
 3 James, *Hawthorne,* 85.
 4 Nathaniel Hawthorne, *The Marble Faun* (Columbus: Ohio State University Press, 1968), 3.

5 James, *Letters,* 2:345. For a thorough contextualization of James's interpretation, see Thaddeo K. Babiiha, *The James-Hawthorne Relation: Bibliographical Essays* (Boston: G. K. Hall, 1980). For a reading of the place of *Hawthorne* in American literary history, see John Carlos Rowe, *The Theoretical Dimensions of Henry James* (Madison: University of Wisconsin Press, 1984), 30–57.

6 James, *Hawthorne,* 3, 85.

7 Alexis de Tocqueville, *Democracy in America,* ed. Phillips Bradley, 2 vols. (New York: Knopf, 1956), 2:77.

8 For James's early contempt for and later embrace of Whitman's work, see *Walt Whitman: The Critical Heritage,* ed. Milton Hindus (London: Routledge, 1971), 110–14, 259–60.

9 Quoted in Babiiha, *The James-Hawthorne Relation,* 13. James's feelings about America are, of course, complex and ambivalent. My purpose here is to isolate one ambivalence in order to introduce a discussion of James's notion of American thinking. Aside from biographical material and James's own numerous essays and reviews, recent critical treatments of James's ideas about America from a sociocultural perspective include Ross Posnock, *The Trial of Curiosity: Henry James, William James, and the Challenge of Modernity* (New York: Oxford University Press, 1991); Virginia C. Fowler, *Henry James's American Girl* (Madison: University of Wisconsin Press, 1984); and Michael Anesko, *"Friction with the Market": Henry James and the Profession of Authorship* (New York: Oxford University Press, 1986).

10 James, *Letters,* 1:77.

11 Horace Kallen, *Cultural Pluralism and the American Idea* (Philadelphia: University of Pennsylvania Press, 1956), 60.

12 This categorical term should not be taken as a general capsule of James's thinking. It applies only to the problematic at hand. For recent extensive discussions of Jamesian consciousness, see Rowe, *Theoretical Dimensions,* 194–256; Donna Przybylowicz, *Desire and Repression: The Dialectic of Self and Other in the Late Works of Henry James* (University: University of Alabama Press, 1986); Sharon Cameron, *Thinking in Henry James* (Chicago: University of Chicago Press, 1990); and Paul Armstrong, *The Phenomenology of Henry James* (Chapel Hill: University of North Carolina Press, 1983).

Ezra Pound describes James's fundamental motive in the later writings as a "labour[ing] to create means of communication." For Pound, while the Adamic consciousness seeks to communicate with raw, undifferentiated nature, Jamesian thinking seeks to communicate with that which is different and to do so in such a way that the communication preserves the difference: "And this communication is not a levelling, it is not an elimination of differences. It is a recognition of differences, of the right of differences to exist, of interest in finding things different" (*Literary Essays of Ezra Pound,* ed. T. S. Eliot [New York: New Directions, 1954], 298).

13 Henry James, *The American* (New York: Scribners, 1907), 27, 31, 32, 32, 45, 32.

14 James, *Letters,* 1:77.

15 Quoted in F. O. Matthiessen, *The James Family* (New York: Knopf, 1947), 339. For more critical commentary on the brothers' relationship, see Posnock, *The Trial of Curiosity,* passim; Richard Hocks, *Henry James and Pragmatistic Thought* (Chapel Hill: University of North Carolina Press, 1974); and Howard Feinstein, *Becoming William James* (Ithaca, N.Y.: Cornell University Press, 1984).

16 William James, *Pragmatism* (Cambridge, Mass.: Harvard University Press, 1978), 32. Quotations are taken from volumes in the standard edition published by Harvard University Press under the general editorship of Frederick H. Burkhardt and appearing as follows: *Essays in Radical Empiricism* (1976); *A Pluralistic Universe* (1977); *Essays in Philosophy* (1978); *The Will to Believe* (1979); *The Principles of Psychology* (1983); and *Manuscript Essays and Notes* (1988). Subsequent documentation will be given in the text.

On the pragmatic idea of thinking as instrumental, see Sidney Hook, *The Metaphysics of Pragmatism* (Chicago: Open Court, 1927), especially the discussion of the instrument as "a monument to a felt lack in existence" (p. 22) and as "the safeguard and mainstay of objectivity" (p. 36). An ambitious extension of pragmatism's instrumentalism is the work of Nicholas Rescher, particularly the texts *Methodological Pragmatism: A Systems-Theoretic Approach to the Theory of Knowledge* (Oxford: Basil Blackwell, 1977) and *A System of Pragmatic Idealism: Human Knowledge in Idealistic Perspective* (Princeton, N.J.: Princeton University Press, 1992). Rescher's interpretation of pragmatism is especially pertinent to this study in that it focuses directly on cognition as the crux of pragmatic behavior and characterizes cognition in explicitly methodological terms. Other general studies of pragmatism that highlight its instrumentalism include S. Morris Eames, *Pragmatic Naturalism: An Introduction* (Carbondale: Southern Illinois University Press, 1977); John E. Smith, *Purpose and Thought: The Meaning of Pragmatism* (New Haven, Conn.: Yale University Press, 1978); Rorty, *Consequences of Pragmatism;* Joseph Margolis, *Pragmatism without Foundations: Reconciling Realism and Relativism* (Oxford: Basil Blackwell, 1986); and Sandra Rosenthal, *Speculative Pragmatism* (Amherst: University of Massachusetts Press, 1986). For an analytic philosophy type treatment of pragmatism, see A. J. Ayer, *The Origins of Pragmatism: Studies in the Philosophy of Charles Sanders Peirce and William James* (San Francisco: Freeman, Cooper, 1968). Along similar lines, see *William James: "Pragmatism" in Focus,* ed. Doris Olin (London: Routledge,

1992), which contains important essays by G. E. Moore and Bertrand Russell, both of which critique James's definition of truth. For a well-known indictment of instrumentalism, see Max Horkheimer, *Eclipse of Reason* (1947; reprint, New York: Seabury, 1974).

17 Lentricchia, *Ariel and the Police,* 106. For recent readings of James that propose to unveil the political background and/or implications of his arguments, see Posnock, *The Trial of Curiosity;* Frank Lentricchia, "Philosophers of Modernism at Harvard, circa 1900," *South Atlantic Quarterly* 89 (1990): 787–834, and *Ariel and the Police,* 104–33; West, *The American Evasion of Philosophy,* 54–68; Richard Poirier, *The Renewal of Literature: Emersonian Reflections* (New York: Random House, 1987), 42–66; and George Cotkin, *William James: Public Philosopher* (Baltimore: Johns Hopkins University Press, 1990). In general, these interpretations choose "to locate James and his philosophy within the social, political, and cultural realms" (Cotkin, *William James,* 5), assuming that these realms contextualize James's ideas and help explain their genesis, although the question of how the politics of pragmatism explicates the meaning of pragmatism remains generally unaddressed by these texts. Also, one might note that, Posnock and Cotkin excepted, these texts quote sparingly from James's corpus and rather hastily align James's complex philosophical formulations with set political positions.

18 While the scholarly literature that broaches James's pragmatism makes up a significant segment of contemporary cultural criticism, studies relating his pragmatism to a philosophy of consciousness have been no less numerous and often more rigorous and comprehensive. These include Charlene Haddock Seigfried, *William James's Radical Reconstruction of Philosophy* (Albany: State University of New York Press, 1990); Gerald E. Myers, *William James: His Life and Thought* (New Haven, Conn.: Yale University Press, 1986); Ellen Kappy Suckiel, *The Pragmatic Philosophy of William James* (Notre Dame, Ind.: University of Notre Dame Press, 1982); Marcus Peter Ford, *William James's Philosophy: A New Perspective* (Amherst: University of Massachusetts Press, 1982); Daniel Bjork, *William James: The Center of His Vision* (New York: Columbia University Press, 1988); Hilary Putnam, *Realism with a Human Face,* ed. James Conant (Cambridge, Mass.: Harvard University Press, 1990), 217–51; and T. L. S. Sprigge, *James and Bradley: American Truth and British Reality* (Chicago: Open Court, 1993).

For detailed phenomenological readings of James, see Hans Linschoten, *On the Way toward a Phenomenological Psychology: The Psychology of William James,* trans. Amedeo Giorgi (Pittsburgh: Duquesne University Press, 1968); Bruce Wilshire, *William James and Phenomenology: A Study of "The Principles of Psychology"* (Bloomington: Indiana University Press, 1968); John Wild, *The Radical*

Empiricism of William James (New York: Doubleday, 1969); Richard Stevens, *James and Husserl: The Foundations of Meaning* (The Hague: Martinus Nijhoff, 1974); and James M. Edie, *William James and Phenomenology* (Bloomington: Indiana University Press, 1987). Each of these studies finds in James a form of pre-Husserlian insight, one bearing on the intentional structure of consciousness.

19 Regarding the putative givenness of sensation, James says, "No one ever had a simple sensation by itself. Consciousness . . . is of a teeming multiplicity of objects and relations, and what we call simple sensations are results of discriminative attention" (*Principles*, 219). A sensation is an abstraction, a stabilizing of those relations constituting a sensation as such so that the sense content may be foregrounded. James's interpretation of sensation borrows heavily from, as well as criticizing often, the prevailing psychological theories of Spencer, Alexander Bain, and Shadworth Hodgson. For example, James takes his "stream of consciousness" metaphor from Bain, who refers to "the current of thoughts or ideas" and "the stream of images and recollections coming into the present view of the mind" (*The Emotions and the Will* [London: John W. Parker & Son, 1859], 409). However, as James notes in a footnote (*Principles*, 237–38), Bain interprets the stream as a "series of distinct ideas," not as a continuous current of thinking.

20 James devotes an entire chapter to the process of attention. For close analyses of James's concept, see Wild, *Radical Empiricism*, 116–28; Myers, *William James*, 181–214; and Siegfried, *Radical Reconstruction*, 84–89. The idea that mind converts sensation into a rational, coherent process through a focus of attention can also be found extensively in Bain's work.

21 Nietzsche, *The Will to Power*, 330. Nietzsche's claim is less unusual than it might sound, for Bain (in both *The Emotions and the Will* and *The Senses and the Intellect* [London: John W. Parker & Son, 1855]) and Spencer (in *The Principles of Psychology* [1855; New York: D. Appleton, 1897]) also link "attention" to "will."

22 In a series of notes on Hegelism (published in *Manuscript Essays and Notes*), James aligns this contentment with the emotive effect of any sublation. He writes, "It carries with it a strong intellectual elation, as if one had now been everywhere, and surrounded all possibilities, included one's own other, and by ascending to a higher region altogether possessed all the region below, and seen through & transcended its oppositions" (p. 230). Here, as in "The Sentiment of Rationality," James goes on to affirm the provisional nature of such inclusions. This assertion of an emotional basis for assertions of transcendence was a briskly debated topic at the time James first began publishing his pragmatism essays (from 1898 on). Because the issue of transcendence lay at the center of contemporary idealism (represented mainly by Bradley), James's emotive

characterization became an object for numerous idealist attacks. See Sprigge, *James and Bradley*, passim; and the lengthy exchanges between James and Dewey and their idealist antagonists in *Mind* and *Journal of Philosophy, Psychology, and Scientific Methods* during the years 1903–9.

23 Precise philosophical discussions of James on the consciousness of objects can be found in Edie, *William James and Phenomenology*, passim; Seigfried, *Radical Reconstruction*, 67–71; Myers, *William James*, 247–55; and Sprigge, *James and Bradley*, 50–65. Again, for a precursor analysis, see Bain on "specialized sensation" and cognition (*The Emotions and the Will*, 636).

24 Note Kant's comments on the compatibility of limitation and progress: "In mathematics and natural science, human reason admits of limits but not of bounds, viz., that something indeed lies outside it, at which it can never arrive, but not that it will at any point find completion in its internal progress" (*Prolegomena to Any Future Metaphysics* [Indianapolis: Hackett, 1977]).

25 "Ontologic wonder" is not to be confused with the "ontological wonder-sickness" cited in a later piece published as a chapter in *The Will to Believe* under the same title, "The Sentiment of Rationality." The latter chapter extensively revises the first and last pages of the earlier essay into eight introductory pages. The early version first appeared in *Mind* in 1879 and is placed by the editors of the Harvard edition of James's works in *Essays in Philosophy*. (James's editors call the later version "a new essay, independent of its forebears" [*Will*, 326]). In the later version, James defines *ontologic wonder-sickness* as "the craving for further explanation" (p. 63). But *ontologic wonder* is precisely the absence of such craving. If ontologic wonder "strives for an understanding of the whole universe" (Seigfried, *Radical Reconstruction*, 33), it does so by pondering the universe's limits, that is, the universe's barely conceivable relation to the nonuniverse. In the earlier essay, this rumination is not a form of sterility, although the latter piece implies it is, wonder there being a purely "theoretic contemplation" that stifles the practical inquiries hinted at in the earlier essay's final sentences. Posnock makes this sterility a starting point for his discussion of James (*The Trial of Curiosity*, 27, 39–41), although he confines his analysis to the later version—the one in *The Will to Believe*—and does not note any of the complications surrounding the word *wonder* in the earlier version. Indeed, Posnock's citation of "The Sentiment of Rationality" is misleading: he says, "Written in 1877 and published in the year he began teaching philosophy, the essay's opening sentence asks why 'philosophers philosophize at all?'" (p. 39). Posnock goes on to quote from the essay, but he uses the later version for his citations, not the one written in 1877. It seems as if he considers the two versions identical—in this case, a sloppy oversight and a misrepresentation of bibliographic facts.

In *The Wilderness and the City: American Classical Philosophy as a Moral Quest* (Amherst: University of Massachusetts Press, 1982), 78–80, Michael A. Weinstein also cites only the later essay in his commentary on Jamesian "wonder," briefly linking it to Heidegger's analysis of dread and nothingness. Heidegger's articulation of how and why one experiences the "strangeness of beings" appears in "What Is Metaphysics?" an essay turning on a single metaphysical event: "the revelation of the nothing" (*Basic Writings,* ed. and trans. David Farrell Krell [New York: Harper & Row, 1977], 111).

Although Bain's work does not directly enter into James's argument in "The Sentiment of Rationality," Bain does devote a few sections of *The Emotions and the Will* to the experience of wonder. He writes: "With reference, then, to the *object* of wonder we say in general that anything that very much surpasses or deviates from our habitual experience calls forth the excitement. . . . The rupture of this accustomed continuity of events causes a certain shock which we denominate surprise, wonder, or astonishment" (p. 67).

26 Perhaps on occasion James affirms identity only to avoid using the self-destructing language of negative theology or intuitionism, a language resigned to its own failure and attractive to his metaphysics of experience. One might argue that James's desire for stability leads him to use a language of fixities to describe the flux, leaving him open to Posnock's (and others') charge that he "appears to reify reality into a graspable essence" (*The Trial of Curiosity,* 108). Yet James's awareness of the contradictions into which his language leads him is fairly clear. For example, he explicitly notes how the concept of flux contradicts itself: "The very conception of flux itself is an absolutely changeless meaning in the mind: it signifies just that one thing, flux, immovably" (*Principles,* 442). Earlier, in discussing the stream of thought, he notes how "language works against our perception of the truth" (p. 234) by substantiating a portion of experience and treating it as simple and independent: "We name our thoughts simply, each after its thing, as if each knew its own thing and nothing else." This is a grammatical violence to the continuity of thinking, a repression of the relational meaning of things. But, while James continues to speak in substantives, he also continues to interrogate his language. In *A Pluralistic Universe,* in trying to describe "the continuity of experience," he confesses, "I am tiring myself and you . . . by vainly seeking to describe by concepts and words what I say at the same time exceeds either conceptualization or verbalization" (p. 131). This is a sophisticated formulation in that it positions pure continuity as an excess, one that has meaning only in relation to what it exceeds. Although neither mastered by nor created by language, it is a function of language (or conceptuality), entering into thinking only as the nondiscrete alterity of any discrete thought. Such moments in James's presentation, then,

are not just stylistic hesitations. They are crucial to his outlining the limits of thinking.

27 This modern mind is, in fact, James's mind, as Bergson's testimonial description of it confirms: "He was stirred by an immense unrest, and went from science to science . . . tense over great problems, heedless of anything else, forgetful of himself. All his life he observed, experimented, meditated. And as if he had not done enough, he still dreamed, as he fell into his last slumber, of extraordinary experiments and superhuman efforts by which he could continue even beyond death to work with us for the greater good of science, and the greater glory of truth" (*The Creative Mind,* trans. Mabelle L. Andison [New York: Philosophical Library, 1946], 260). For more on James and Bergson, see Sprigge, *James and Bradley,* 186–91. It should be noted that numerous books and articles published on pragmatism early in the century place Bergson squarely at the center of the pragmatic movement and ally him with James. See, e.g., Ralph Barton Perry, *Present Philosophical Tendencies* (New York: Longmans, Green, 1912); William Caldwell, *Pragmatism and Idealism* (London: Adam & Charles Black, 1913); and John T. Driscoll, *Pragmatism and the Problem of the Idea* (New York: Longmans, Green, 1915). One exception to this alignment of James and Bergson is Horace Kallen's *William James and Henri Bergson: A Study in Contrasting Theories of Life* (Chicago: University of Chicago Press, 1914).

28 For a typical example of discussions of pragmatism's political implications, see Cornel West, "Theory, Pragmatism, Politics," in *Pragmatism: From Progressivism to Postmodernism,* ed. Robert Hollinger and David Depew (Westport, Conn.: Praeger, 1995), 314–25.

3 Peirce's Logic of Pragmatic Inference

1 Linschoten (*Toward a Phenomenological Psychology*), Wilshire (*William James and Phenomenology*), Stevens (*James and Husserl*), and Edie (*William James and Phenomenology*) all explore James's understanding of intentionality and claim for James an insight that Husserl would develop soon after. Edie writes that "Husserl's library, preserved at Louvain, contains most of James's major works and two reprints James sent to Husserl. Only the *Principles of Psychology,* however, and one of the reprints, 'The Knowing of Things Together,' contain marks and marginal notes which indicate that they were read intensively" (p. 23). Edie goes on to note Husserl's own public acknowledgment of James's influence, e.g., Husserl's noting that his concept of the "horizontal structure of experience" derives in part from James's concept of "fringes of consciousness."

2 Quotations from Peirce are taken from the ongoing *Writings of Charles Sanders Peirce: A Chronological Edition* (cited as *W* by volume and page number), ed.

Max Fisch et al., 5 vols. (Bloomington: Indiana University Press, 1982–); and *The Collected Papers of Charles Sanders Peirce* (cited as *CP* by volume and paragraph), 8 vols., vols. 1–6 ed. Charles Hartshorne and Paul Weiss, vols. 7–8 ed. Arthur W. Burks (Cambridge, Mass.: Harvard University Press, 1931–35, 1958). Occasional citations come from *Semiotic and Significs: The Correspondence of Charles S. Peirce and Victoria Lady Welby*, ed. Charles Hardwick (Bloomington: Indiana University Press, 1977).

3 Peirce's ethical assertions about the benefits of community awareness as opposed to individualized thinking are scattered throughout his writings. For ethical readings that focus on Peirce's community ideas, see West, *The American Evasion of Philosophy*, 43–54; Weinstein, *The Wilderness and the City*, 49–67; and Jurgen Habermas, *Knowledge and Human Interests*, trans. Jeremy J. Shapiro (Boston: Beacon, 1971), 91–131. These analyses focus on how a narrowly individualistic version of pragmatism can lead to greed (West, *The American Evasion of Philosophy*, 46) or to a spurious presumption of neutrality (Habermas, *Knowledge and Human Interests*, 129). They also distinguish James's more ethically oriented version of pragmatism from Peirce's, in agreement with Peirce's frequent assertion of scientific inquiry's nonethical purpose: "Restricting myself . . . to scientific reasoning, I need not go behind the recognized purpose of science, which stops at knowledge," which is to say, short of "the question of pure ethics" (*CP*, 7.201); "the real character of science is destroyed as soon as it is made an adjunct to conduct" (*CP*, 1.55). For a survey of Peirce's (and James's and Dewey's) political ideas, see the chapter entitled "Moral, Social, and Political Theories: The Pragmatists" in Robert J. Roth's *British Empiricism and American Pragmatism: New Directions and Neglected Arguments* (New York: Fordham University Press, 1993).

For discussions of Peirce's disagreements with James about the nature of cognition see W. B. Gallie, *Peirce and Pragmatism* (Westport, Conn.: Greenwood, 1966); Karl-Otto Apel, *Charles Sanders Peirce: From Pragmatism to Pragmaticism*, trans. John Michael Krois (Amherst: University of Massachusetts Press, 1981); and Robert S. Corrington, *An Introduction to C. S. Peirce: Philosopher, Semiotician, and Ecstatic Naturalist* (Lanham, Md.: Rowman & Littlefield, 1993). Apart from these works, other general studies of Peirce's concept of cognition that bear on the present argument are Murray G. Murphey, *The Development of Peirce's Philosophy* (Cambridge, Mass.: Harvard University Press, 1961); William H. Davis, *Peirce's Epistemology* (The Hague: Martinus Nijhoff, 1972); Joseph L. Esposito, *Evolutionary Metaphysics: The Development of Peirce's Theory of Categories* (Athens: Ohio University Press, 1980); Christopher Hookway, *Peirce* (London: Routledge & Kegan Paul, 1985) (a superior explication); Vincent M. Colapietro, *Peirce's Approach to the Self: A Semiotic Perspec-*

tive on Human Subjectivity (Albany: State University of New York Press, 1989); and Carl R. Hausman, *Charles S. Peirce's Evolutionary Philosophy* (Cambridge: Cambridge University Press, 1993).

4 In *W,* 1:498, Peirce seems to describe an interpersonal attitude that might seem to posit a "social impulse" as the basis of human being: "When I communicate my thoughts and my sentiments to a friend with whom I am in full sympathy, so that my feelings pass into him and I am conscious of what he feels, do I not live in his brain as well as in my own—most literally? . . . But that he truly has this outreaching identity . . . is the true and exact expression of the fact of sympathy, fellow feeling." *Communication, sympathy, fellow feeling*—these terms suggest that a personal identity may find its completion only in gestures of "outreaching." However, if the outreaching identity exists only insofar as it does the outreaching, then it is the *act,* not some impulse doing the acting, that makes up man. One must guard against substituting a transpersonal psychic substance for a personal psychic substance, a shift that expands the datum of psychology beyond an individual mind but leaves the psychologistic basis of thinking unquestioned.

5 Peirce's definition of *hypothesis* appears in most of his discussions of methods of reasoning. See, e.g., *CP,* 1.120, 247, 369; throughout *CP,* vol. 7; *W,* 2:43–48, 238–39, 265–66; *W,* 3:4–6, 332–38. For his related concepts of *abduction* and *retroduction,* see *CP,* 1.68, 7.218–22. Critical analyses of Peirce on hypothesis include Murphey, *The Development of Peirce's Philosophy,* 113–16; Gallie, *Peirce and Pragmatism,* 97–103; Apel, *Charles Sanders Peirce,* 40–44; Davis, *Peirce's Epistemology,* 22–49 (Davis refers Peirce's "hypothesis" to Hume's analysis of induction); Hookway, *Peirce,* 222–29; and C. F. Delaney, *Science, Knowledge, and Mind: A Study in the Philosophy of C. S. Peirce* (Notre Dame, Ind.: Notre Dame University Press, 1993), 38–42, 124–26. For Peirce on induction and scientific method, see Isaac Levi's "Induction According to Peirce," Joseph S. Ullian's "On Peirce on Induction: A Response to Isaac Levi," Nicholas Rescher's "Peirce on the Validation of Science," and Cornelius J. Delaney's "Peirce on the Reliability of Science: A Response to Rescher," all in the collection *Peirce and Contemporary Thought: Philosophical Inquiries,* ed. Kenneth Laine Ketner (New York: Fordham University Press, 1995). The collection also has essays by Putnam, Quine, Eco, Sebeok, Habermas, and Apel. On Peirce's theories of induction and how they relate to the British empiricist tradition, see Roth, *British Empiricism and American Pragmatism,* 37–44. For a more technical account of pragmatic induction in general and justification in particular, see the opening five chapters of Rescher's *Methodological Pragmatism.*

6 In *W,* 2:208, Peirce offers a typical statement of why cognition belongs to any definition of reality: "Over against any cognition, there is an unknown but

knowable reality; but over against all possible cognition, there is only the self-contradictory. In short, *cognizability* (in its widest sense) and *being* are not merely metaphysically the same, but are synonymous terms." This is not to say that an incognizable reality does not exist (since that would be, in however limited a way, to cognize it) but rather to claim that the idea of an incognizable reality makes no sense, is self-contradictory. As Apel puts it, "A philosophy which conceived knowledge to be representation by signs . . . must reject as meaningless the concept of the absolutely incognizable" (*Charles Sanders Peirce*, 44).

7   Many discussions of the interpretant—e.g., Gallie, *Peirce and Pragmatism*, 118–30; Ayer, *The Origins of Pragmatism*, 119–28 (although Ayer misconstrues Peirce's notion by seeing an interpretant as extrinsic to, not constitutive of, the sign); and Hookway, *Peirce*, 121–27—treat the term as a semiotic function, an inference that most of Peirce's writings certainly justify. But, given the quotations presented above, Peirce's interpretant has a cognitive function as well, one amounting, not to an aftereffect of a completed cognition, but to a reference that renders a cognition cognizable.

8   Compare Peirce's definition of the sign in a letter to Lady Welby, where *corresponding* serves the purposes that *same* does: "A sign therefore is an object which is in relation to its object on the one hand and to an interpretant on the other in such a way as to bring the interpretant into a relation to the object corresponding to its own relation to the object" (*Semiotic and Significs*, 32). Note that the correspondence is between two relations, not between a sign and an object. A few years earlier, in *Dictionary of Philosophy and Psychology*, ed. J. M. Baldwin (New York: Macmillan, 1902), Peirce also used *sameness* to signify a correspondence of "references." In the entry on "Sign," he defines it as "anything which determines something else (its *interpretant*) to refer to an object to which itself refers (its *object*) in the same way, the interpretant becoming a sign in turn."

9   Of course, with the inference of a subject pole comes that of an object pole, the latter being due to the same recognition of error and corrigibility that led to the hypothesis of selfhood: "And what do we mean by the real? It is a conception which we must first have had when we discovered that there was an unreal, an illusion; that is, when we first corrected ourselves" (*W*, 2:239).

10 Extensive analyses of Peirce's fallibilism include Davis, *Peirce's Epistemology*, 87–107 (Davis relates Peirce's position to Humean skepticism); Peter Skagestad, *The Road of Inquiry* (New York: Columbia University Press, 1981), passim; Hookway, *Peirce*, passim; and Delaney, *Science, Knowledge, and Mind*, 66–70, 106–11. While Peirce's notion permeates his discussions of scientific method, the above quotations reveal that it also is necessary to explain the evolution of cognition.

11 Peirce's notion of reality is too complex to go into here (a section in "How to Make Our Ideas Clear" contains his clearest explication of the concept). However, one aspect of it may be easily singled out at this point: that "the Real is such that whatever is true of it is not true because some individual person's thought or some individual group of persons' thought attributes its predicate to its subject, but is true, no matter what any person or group of persons may think *about* it" (*Semiotic and Significs,* 116). That is, "that whose characters are independent of how you or I think is an external reality" (*W,* 3:271). Now, because there is no such thing as an incognizable reality, the only way to gauge independence is if two minds agree in the object of their cognitions and then attribute that object's truth to something other than each mind's individual act of thinking. Reality is, thus, a matter of consensus, an "ultimate conclusion" that "though independent of this or that mind is not independent of mind in general" (*W,* 3:8). Peirce concedes that, being process oriented and community dependent, "the real is something ideal and never actually exists" (p. 9). But its ideality does not invalidate it, and the fact that it explains agreement and collaboration without having recourse to an absolutely independent entity renders it highly serviceable to scientific study.

Peirce's lengthiest statement on the issue of reality's independence appears in his review of Fraser's edition of Berkeley (*W* 2:462–87), which links Peirce's realism to that of scholastic thinkers, mainly Duns Scotus. For a book-length treatment of Peirce and scholasticism, see John F. Boler, *Charles Peirce and Scholastic Realism: A Study of Peirce's Relation to John Duns Scotus* (Seattle: University of Washington Press, 1963). See also Max H. Fisch, "Peirce's Progress from Nominalism toward Realism," in *Peirce, Semiotic, and Pragmatism: Essays by Max H. Fisch,* ed. Kenneth Laine Ketner and Christian J. W. Kloesel (Bloomington: Indiana University Press, 1986), 184–200.

12 It must be remembered that what inquiring minds come closer and closer to is not an already existent truth; rather, truth is what is predicated of whatever minds come closer and closer to, their approach being measured by how many minds assent to the results of the inquiry. The "predestined true conclusion" to which Peirce often refers owes its fatefulness not to some occult agent in the object of inquiry forcing minds to think of it in a certain "true" way (see *W,* 3:44–45). Rather, fate lies in the nature of the communal inquiry, the general tendency of inquirers to reach agreement. It is a community function, not an ontological entity. Peirce does say that "truth has that compulsive nature" toward which "any person you please would come if he pursued his inquiries far enough" (*Semiotic and Significs,* 73). But, in order to prevent someone from taking his principle of "ultimate opinion" as itself an assertion of fate or an "infallible truth," he limits the principle to analytic status: "It is a mere defini-

tion. I do not say that it is infallibly true that there is any belief to which a person would come if he were to carry his inquiries far enough. I only say that that alone is what I call Truth. I cannot infallibly know that there is any Truth" (p. 73).

13 The citation on individuality and falsity appears in a note to "How to Make Our Ideas Clear" that Peirce added in 1893. On Peirce and individuals, see Gresham Riley, "Peirce's Theory of Individuals," *Transactions of the Charles Sanders Peirce Society* 10 (1974): 135–63.

14 Peirce demonstrates the contradictory nature of this concept numerous times in his logical analyses of the *ding an sich* as an "incognizable cognizable" (see *W,* 2:190–91, 208, 213, 3:319).

15 Peirce considers this leap one of the roots of psychologism, one especially pernicious in that it makes the psyche into an ultimate thing from which other things are inferred, thus subsuming logic within the purview of psychology. In granting an individual psyche priority over inferential thinking, psychologists reduce logic to one species of reasoning. But, for Peirce, logic does not simply construct principles of valid argumentation. It constitutes a description of mind's rational workings. As Richard Whately claims in *Elements of Logic* (1826; reprint, Delmar, N.Y.: Scholars' Facsimiles & Reprints, 1975), a text Peirce says he devoured when he was twelve years old: "Logic has usually been considered by these objectors as professing to furnish a *peculiar* method of reasoning, instead of a method of analyzing that mental process which must *invariably* take place in all correct reasoning" (p. 11). A few pages later, Whately writes, "In every instance in which we *reason* . . . a certain process takes place in the mind, which is one and the same in all cases, provided it be correctly conducted" (p. 18). What logic does is explain the principles behind that process, for logic is not merely an art of reasoning but *the* act of reasoning. In another text influencing Peirce's conception of logic, George Boole's *An Investigation into the Laws of Thought* (New York: Dover, 1854), the author echoes Whately in proposing "to investigate the fundamental laws of those operations of the mind by which reasoning is performed" (p. 3). In identifying correct reasoning with logic, in saying that a faulty cognition equals an error of logic, Boole and Whately make the study of mind a matter, not of determining a psychology of motives, faculties, adaptations, and so on, but of extrapolating a logic of cognition. For more on Peirce and psychologism, see Hookway, *Peirce,* 15–18, 52–56; and Colapietro, *Peirce's Approach to the Self,* 49–60.

16 In a letter to Lady Welby, Peirce speaks of persons in the same substantial way that he does self and object when he defines the sign: "I define a Sign as anything which is so determined by something else, called its Object, and so

determined an effect upon a person, which effect I call its Interpretant, that the latter is thereby mediately determined by the former" (*Semiotic and Significs,* 80–81). But, to prevent Welby from assuming that persons lie outside or before the semiotic process, Peirce continues by claiming, "My insertion of 'upon a person' is a sop to Cerberus, because I despair of making my own broader conception understood" (p. 81). What Peirce probably means is that Cartesian habits of thinking are so sedimented in contemporary thought that even sophisticated thinkers have a hard time conceiving persons as inferred entities, not as given, self-present entities.

Epilogue

1 For a detailed account of the development and composition of "How to Make Our Ideas Clear," see Max Fisch's introduction to vol. 3 of the *Writings,* esp. pp. xxix–xxxvii.

2 Rorty's depreciative comments on Peirce in *Consequences of Pragmatism* (pp. 160–61) and elsewhere have had the effect of minimizing neopragmatic commentary on Peirce in the last twenty years. The essays in *Against Theory* contain only slight allusions to Peirce's work. In their respective writings, Fish, Lentricchia, Gunn, Bloom, and Posnock rarely refer to Peirce. Richard Poirier has nothing to say about Peirce in *Poetry and Pragmatism* (Cambridge, Mass.: Harvard University Press, 1992) (there is no way to reconcile Poirier's simplistic understanding of pragmatism as "linguistic skepticism" with Peirce's unskeptical position). Gary Wihl's *The Contingency of Theory: Pragmatism, Expressivism, and Deconstruction* (New Haven, Conn.: Yale University Press, 1994) has not a single reference to Peirce (or to James or Dewey!) in its index. Many of the essays in *Reading Rorty: Critical Responses to "Philosophy and the Mirror of Nature" (and Beyond)* (ed. Alan R. Malachowski [Oxford: Basil Blackwell, 1990]) touch on neopragmatist ideas (some titles are "Redefining Philosophy as Literature," "The Priority of Democracy to Philosophy," and "Conversational Politics"), but the collection contains only two references to Peirce. Such nonresponses constitute more than just a misunderstanding and suggest that a larger study of Peirce and neopragmatism is warranted. For sharp critical analyses that argue Rorty's *mis*interpretation of Peirce and "old" pragmatism, see the essays by Charles Hartshorne, Richard Bernstein, James Gouinlock, and Susan Haack in *Rorty and Pragmatism: The Philosopher Responds to His Critics,* ed. Herman J. Saatkamp Jr. (Nashville: Vanderbilt University Press, 1995). For a witty contrast of Rorty and Peirce, see Haack's "Peirce and Rorty: A Conversation," *Partisan Review* 1 (1997): 91–107.

3 Although these statements were written long after the cognition papers and "How to Make Our Ideas Clear," Peirce's thought on this particular issue of pragmatism's circumscription to conceptual analysis is continuous throughout his writings.

4 Gunn, *Thinking across the American Grain,* 4.

5 Lentricchia, *Criticism and Social Change,* 3.

6 See the conclusion of West's *The American Evasion of Philosophy.*

7 Rorty, *Philosophy and the Mirror of Nature,* 360.

8 Peirce insists again and again on this distinction between doing and understanding what it is you are doing. For example: "We thus see that the act of assertion is an act of a totally different nature from the act of apprehending the meaning of the proposition and we cannot expect that any analysis of what assertion is (or any analysis of what *judgment* or *belief* is, if that act is at all allied to assertion), should throw any light at all on the widely different question of what the apprehension of the meaning of a proposition is" (*CP,* 5.30). See also Peirce's criticism of "the doctrine that to feel and to be aware of the feeling are the same thing" (*W,* 2:37).

9 We should note, however, that Peirce has little more than contempt for, as he calls it, the "new analysis that the True is simply that in cognition which is Satisfactory" (*CP,* 5.555). In his eyes, it hardly merits philosophical consideration: "As to this doctrine, if it is meant that True and Satisfactory are synonyms, it strikes me that it is not so much a doctrine of philosophy as it is a new contribution to English lexicography." For more of Peirce's comments on the separation of scientific inquiry from personal, ethical, and political concerns, see his 1898 Cambridge Conference Lectures, recently published as *Reasoning and the Logic of Things,* ed. Kenneth Laine Ketner (Cambridge, Mass.: Harvard University Press, 1992), esp. pp. 108–13.

10 See, e.g., Rorty, *Consequences of Pragmatism,* 166.

11 Fish's term—see *Is There a Text in This Class,* 308.

12 See Rorty, *Consequences of Pragmatism,* 13–17.

Index

Mark Bauerlein is Associate Professor of English at Emory University.

Library of Congress Cataloging-in-Publication Data
Bauerlein, Mark.
The pragmatic mind : explorations in the psychology of belief / Mark Bauerlein.
   p.   cm.—(New Americanists)
Includes bibliographical references and index.
ISBN 0-8223-2004-5 (cloth : alk. paper). — ISBN 0-8223-2013-4 (paper : alk. paper)
1. Pragmatism—History.   2. Psychology—United States—Philosophy—History.   3. Emerson, Ralph Waldo, 1803–1882.   4. Peirce, Charles S. (Charles Sanders), 1839–1914.   5. James, William, 1842–1910.
I. Title. II. Series.
B832.B36   1997
144'.3'0973—dc21   97-6289